Praise for <u>Baseline Shift</u>

"Not only does this book shine a light on so many new-to-me (and probably new-to-you) stories of women in graphic design, but the stories are told by an incredible crew of contemporary design writers who skillfully make these untold stories accessible to a new audience. *Baseline Shift* is a much-needed book for both inside the design classroom and out."
—Kate Bingaman Burt, illustrator and educator

"There's real irony in how little we collectively know about the women who shaped the medium of graphic communication. *Baseline Shift* showcases the women designers, printers, illustrators, and typesetters who used their skills to drive both industrial and social change, connecting them in a dialogue that illuminates history and resonates in the current day."
—Andi Zeisler, author of *We Were Feminists Once*

"*Baseline Shift* challenges not only what gender, race, and nationality we think of when we say 'graphic designer' but also how the work gets done and what purpose it serves. Designers' paths have long been circumscribed by assumptions that design must strictly serve business (the long-standing default path being climbing the 'studio ladder' and the alienation from craft that entails).

This collection of essays models different ways of existing in the world as a graphic designer. Design's enduring importance in activism, modes of nonhierarchical collaboration modeled by small design collectives, and the empowerment of marginalized groups through outlets like community printshops—these are all part of our inheritance as graphic designers, too.

Telling this more capacious history is an important step toward a future of expanded possibilities for us all."
—Kelli Anderson, author of *This Book Is a Planetarium*

Edited by Briar Levit

Baseline Shift

Untold Stories
of Women
in Graphic
Design History

Princeton Architectural Press
New York

**(Previous spread) The Monotype
Type Design Office in the 1930s.**

Published by
Princeton Architectural Press
202 Warren Street
Hudson, New York 12534
www.papress.com

Editor: Sara Stemen
Designer: Briar Levit
Typefaces: CoFo Sans by Maria Doreuli and Roba by Franziska Weitgruber

Library of Congress Cataloging-in-Publication Data

Names: Levit, Briar, editor.
Title: Baseline shift : untold stories of women in graphic design history /
    edited by Briar Levit.
Description: First edition. | New York : Princeton Architectural Press,
    [2021] | Includes bibliographical references and index. | Summary:
    "Essays examining the lives and work of diverse unsung women through-
out the history of graphic design"— Provided by publisher.
Identifiers: LCCN 2020055367 | ISBN 9781648960062 (hardcover)
Subjects: LCSH: Women commercial artists—Biography.
Classification: LCC NC998 .B375 2021 | DDC 741.6092/2—dc23
LC record available at https://lccn.loc.gov/2020055367

Contents

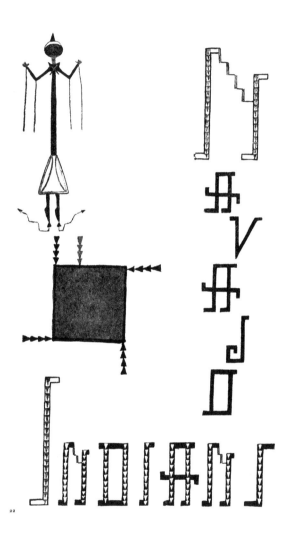

Introduction:
They Were There, Too

The story of graphic design is not tidy and linear, as it is often presented. Our dominant narratives of one art and design movement leading seamlessly to the next can make conceiving the passage of ideas and events more palatable, but can keep us from understanding what is true. Design history is in reality more of a tree with endless branches and roots leading every which way. The narratives we explore in this book of essays form some of the smaller branches on that tree of history. But why do these branches seem small?

In 1994, design historian Martha Scotford established a new framework, based in feminist theory, for looking at graphic design history:

> Neat history is conventional history: a focus on the mainstream activities and work of individual, usually male, designers. Messy history seeks to discover, study and include the variety of alternative approaches and activities that are often part of women designers' professional lives.

Lettering and design by Angel De Cora (Hinook Mahiwi Kilinaka), which draws from Navajo motifs. Opening page of "Navajo" chapter from *The Indians' Book*, compiled by Natalie Curtis, 1907.

"Messy history" would take into account the fact that women have existed under systems with different roles, expectations, and access than those for men. She notes that our study of history must look in the "female frameworks," as she calls them, in which they were able to create, to find, and to understand their contributions. People such as Scotford, Louise Sandhaus (who has an essay featured in this book), Lorraine Wild, and Ellen Lupton jump-started the kind of serious research into women graphic designers and theory about them that this book continues.

If we look at only the most common sources for information, we'd think there were very few notable women designers. And that's because during the brief period that the history of graphic design has been seriously and consistently studied, we have been sold the idea that women graphic designers existed only more recently and in very negligible numbers. According to Martha Scotford, the first edition of Philip Meggs's seminal graphic design history textbook, *Meggs' History of Graphic Design*, mentions 15 women designers and reproduces work of only 9 of them. Recently, associate professor Brandon Waybright analyzed the gender and ethnic makeup of the 2016 edition of *Meggs'* and found 62 women (and 80 BIPOC people) out of a total 594 designers. He clarified that these numbers come "with a strong caveat—that by and large the women and people of color are included in lists with only their name mentioned and no real historic detail."

This approach to chronicling history is a limited one. First, it focuses on the people who dominated. As the old saying goes, "History is written by the victors." In the field of graphic design, the victors were the people who were allowed to go to school, own businesses, join professional organizations where networking and mentoring happen, and enter competitions at will. Not surprisingly, those people were overwhelmingly White men.

The traditional approach to design history also presumes that its students should focus only on artifacts and their formal attributes. While the histories originally published (and reprinted), such as *Meggs'*, sometimes remind us of design's impact giving form to history's content, a contemporary viewing of history (as seen, for example, in Johanna Drucker and Emily McVarish's *Graphic Design History: A Critical Guide*) examines not only form and technique but spends much more time exploring the reasons for the form, and for its existence at all. Many of today's design historians aim to place artifacts in the context of the people who made them, the people who viewed and used them, these people's sociopolitical relationships, and their access to tools and technology. While form remains an exciting subject for investigation, context creates a depth and meaning that can inspire and inform—perhaps to a greater

Katherine Milhous, *Pennsylvania: The Little Red Schoolhouse*, ca. 1936–40, poster.

extent—the work we make today.

The good news is that with a little digging in the places that mainstream journals and professional organizations have forgotten—or, more likely, ignored—researchers are confirming that women of many backgrounds and ethnicities were working with a great deal more regularity and intention in the field of graphic design than most would guess. As discussed in this collection, they ran presses in British colonies—"Quick and Correct Compositors at the Case: Early Colonial Women Printers"—they illustrated books in the studios of culturally cutting-edge Harlem—"A Black Renaissance Woman: Louise E. Jefferson"—and they drew type in the drafting rooms of Europe's major type foundries—"Dora Pritchett, Dora Laing, Patricia Saunders…: The Invisible Women of Monotype's Type Drawing Office." Women designers worked for government offices to get visual messages of safety and patriotism out to the masses—"Women of the Federal Art Project Poster Division"—and they gave a visual voice to the fights for women's liberation—"By Women, For Women: Suffragist Graphic Design"; "Bea Feitler: The *Sir* to *Ms.* Years"; and "In the Beginning, Woman Was the Sun." Some innovated graphic visual languages to help represent their cultures—"'Her Greatest Work Lay in Decorative Design': Angel De Cora, Ho-Chunk Artist, ca. 1869–1919." Others found strength in numbers by creating unions and offering their graphic and production skills to civil rights movements as coconspirators—"Press On!—Feminist Historiography of Print Culture and Collective Organizing"; "Collective Authorship and Shared Process: The

Madame Binh Graphics Collective"; and "Typist to Typesetter: Norma Kitson and Her Red Lion Setters." Not all of the women featured in this book were motivated by activism; some found satisfaction in pursuing a career they loved—"On Söre Popitz, the Bauhaus's Only Known Woman Advertising Designer"; "One for the Books: Ellen Raskin's Design, Lettering, and Illustration"; "Clearing the Fog: Marget Larsen, San Francisco Designer"; and "Betti Broadwater Haft: 'Letterforms Are Sacred to Me.'"

(Above) Söre Popitz, advertisement for Thügina, ca. 1925–33. (Opposite) Bea Feitler, cover designed and illustrated for *Senhor* magazine, July 1960.

Baseline Shift illuminates the stories of these women, offering a counter to the mostly male and White history we've been presented. It offers an expansion of the small canon of women in graphic design that is currently trotted out every time someone asks, "Where are the women in design history?" This book tells stories of auteurs and champions of social justice whose names can we now add to the history. It also tells the stories of nameless women who used design to make change, to do business, and to make a living.

One thing is true. Within these female frameworks, in the shadows and sometimes in full view, despite the challenges and hardships, women were typesetting, printing, designing, illustrating, drafting, and more. They were there, too.

SENHOR

JULHO 1960

CR$ 100,00

"Her Greatest Work Lay in Decorative Design": Angel De Cora, Ho-Chunk Artist, ca. 1869–1919

Linda M. Waggoner

"Angel DeCora, a Winnebago with noble French blood and descended from a line of famous chiefs," wrote Elaine Goodale Eastman in 1919, "was an idealist and an artist to her fingertips."[1] To characterize De Cora (Hinook Mahiwi Kilinaka) as a Native American artist today, however, involves a paradox. Like a shooting star, her trace remains visible, but we no longer perceive her contribution to Native American art. Post–World War II critics found her artwork to be overshadowed by her Western art training, but it is not only her oeuvre that poses a challenge. To contextualize her artwork today, we depend upon a rhetoric of authenticity she herself disseminated.

Opening page of "Kwakiutl," from *The Indians' Book*, compiled by Natalie Curtis, 1907. The lettering, by Angel De Cora (Hinook Mahiwi Kilinaka), draws on Kwakiutl design motifs: "the tail and fin of the whale, the hawk, and the eye-joint," as noted in the text. The drawings, by Klalish (Charles James Nowell), a Kwakiutl Indian, reference the spiritual essence of a grizzly bear and a killer whale.

De Cora was a Ho-Chunk (commonly Winnebago) woman who grew up on the Winnebago reservation in northeastern Nebraska. Born around 1869, she lived in early childhood with her grandparents in a traditional wigwam above the banks of the Missouri River. De Cora grew up observing her tribeswomen create beautiful silverwork, beadwork, and appliqué—at which Ho-Chunk women still excel. Julia De Cora early noticed her sister's artistic bent. "There was the loveliest clay bank where we made all our own toys," she recalled. "Whatever Angel made was done a bit better than we did."[2]

However, De Cora was not honored as a significant Native artist in the National Museum of the American Indian's commemorative book, *Creation's Journey: Native American Identity and Belief* (1994). Her art is not represented, yet the book's text is steeped in her influence, foregrounding concepts of abstraction, discussions of Indian trade economies and Native women, ideals about the American Indian's connection to the land, and the education of Americans about the appropriate use and *authentic* representation of American Indian design elements and symbols.[3]

Although Smithsonian ethnographer John Ewers highlighted De Cora's artistic career in his *Images of a Vanished Life: Plains Indian Drawings from the Collection of the Pennsylvania Academy of the Fine Arts* (1956), he claimed, "There was little in Angel DeCora's mature artistic style to suggest her Indian background."[4] He thought her work too "fine art" influenced to speak to the pictographs of the male Fort Marion Plains ledger book artists his book featured. In 1878 these men attended the first experimental class for Native Americans at Hampton Normal and Agricultural Institute, a freedman's school established in Virginia in 1868. Notably, De Cora, having been abducted by a White recruiter, arrived to enroll in Hampton's "Indian Department" in 1883, just a few years after subscribers to the school's newsletter received free pictographs by the ledger book artists.

Patricia Trenton's *Independent Spirits: Women Painters of the American West, 1890–1945* (1995) acknowledges De Cora as one of three Native American women "who distinguished themselves through their paintings and cultural activities." De Cora's White contemporaries distinguished her even more by declaring her "the first real Indian artist."[5] Yet she did not see herself as exceptional. She believed all Indigenous people were innately gifted artists, particularly in abstract design. Still, De Cora grew up at a time when Indians could *inspire* art but were themselves regarded merely as craft makers.

De Cora's formal art training began in 1892, when she was admitted to the art department of Smith College in Northampton, Massachusetts. She spent her first year studying anatomy, drawing from casts as well as practicing life drawing and still-life painting.

At the end of her second year, a reporter from the *Boston Journal* sang the praises of "the young lady of Indian parentage" who "won the undergraduate prize simply from excellence in cast drawing in charcoal." This was "a distinct departure from the custom observed at the college," noted the reporter, "and, in consequence, Miss DeCora is receiving many encomiums for her marked ability."[6]

De Cora's most influential Smith teacher, Dwight Tryon, emphasized "good draftsmanship" and "clearness and beauty of line," but he also influenced her to paint in his own misty, tonalist style. In 1894, De Cora took courses in composition, landscape sketching, and modeling in clay. When she completed her coursework in June 1896, she received recognition as "one of the most proficient in clay modeling," the skill she'd honed on the banks of the Missouri River. The art department also presented her with "special mention" in color studies, "specially meritorious work" for cast drawing, and honorable mention for a "nocturne sketch" that the judges pronounced "a beautiful thing."[7]

Upon graduation, De Cora submitted her portfolio to Philadelphia's Drexel Institute of Art, Science and Industry. She hoped to study illustration. According to a Hampton teacher, when "the question of 'art for art's sake' or 'art for money's sake'" came up, De Cora's "desire to be independent as soon as possible decided her in favor of taking up illustration as a means to this end."[8] Despite intense competition, Drexel admitted her in September 1896. She took courses from the dynamic Yankee illustrator Howard Pyle, known today as the "father of American illustration" and the mentor of the Brandywine School of artists. Recognizing De Cora's talent, Pyle envisioned a promising career for her in the special niche of Indian illustration and so urged her to sketch and paint her own people.

In June 1897, De Cora journeyed with a Hampton chaperone to the Fort Berthold reservation in North Dakota, home of the Mandan, Hidatsa, and Arikara. "The Indians watched her skill with interest and pride, and became so fond of her and her bright, witty sayings, that she had no trouble in getting any number of people to pose for her," relayed her chaperone. "Some of the portraits she made there of the old chiefs are of great value as well as beauty."[9] A local newspaper further touted, "The wild Indians have always had an aptitude for hieroglyphic or primitive drawing, comparatively few of the educated ones have excelled in the fine arts. Miss DeCora is one of these exceptions and to day stands at the head of her race as a portrait painter."[10]

When De Cora returned to Philadelphia, Pyle encouraged her to write and to illustrate her own stories and introduced her to the publishers of *Harper's Monthly Magazine*. The *Philadelphia Inquirer* reported that De Cora took "Mr. Pyle's costume and illustration classes," where "she progressed very rapidly, making drawings and compositions of a peculiar strength and directness….She is at present at work upon some illustrations for a story of her own shortly to be published in one of the leading American periodicals."[11] In February and November 1899, *Harper's* published "The Sick Child" and "Gray Wolf's Daughter" by "Henook-makhewe-kelenaka (Angel de Cora)." Critics adored her Thunderbird Clan name as well as her poignant and beautifully illustrated semiautobiographical stories.

In 1898, Pyle opened a summer school for his more gifted students along the Brandywine River in Pennsylvania. De Cora won a coveted scholarship. "Look on this, study it, absorb it," Pyle instructed. "Never again will it be the same. If you see it tomorrow, the light will be different and you will be different." As Tryon had urged De Cora to sound the depths of her experience to develop her own style, Pyle espoused a theory of "mental projection," urging students to "paint as you felt," "throw yourself into the picture," and forego "ideas of technique, classical rendition or art school technique."[12] De Cora left little record of that summer, but she left an impression. One student recalled that she "was a genial young woman, ambitious to succeed, but seemingly unable to get away from her native Reservation western life." She observed that when Pyle instructed students to paint "springtime in the country," the "Indian girl's composition would show a hillside cottage embowered in roses and vines; but far in the distance would always be the wide spaces and open prairies of her native haunts."[13] So much for one's own "mental projections."

According to another source, Pyle believed not only that De Cora's gender was a disability, but also, "more unfortunately," that her being "an American Indian" was a handicap. "She was so retiring that she always kept in the background of my classes," he complained. "When I tried to rouse her ambition by telling her how famous she might become, she answered, 'We Indian women are taught that modesty is a woman's chief virtue.'"[14] De Cora's response to his goading reflects the deep cultural chasm between the two, but Pyle was nevertheless bowled over by her talent: "Out of a thousand pupils ten have genius, she's one of the ten," he revealed in a letter. "Of the six compositions she has sent in, every one, if properly painted" and "sent to Paris she would at once become notable."[15]

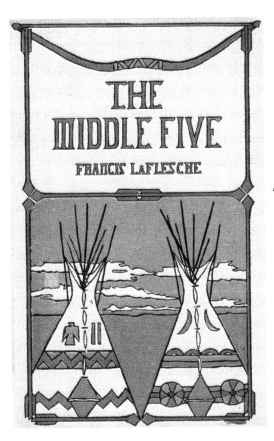

Angel De Cora, cover of *The Middle Five*, Francis La Flesche, 1900.

Nevertheless, De Cora became aware of "certain deficiencies" in her art training and decided to go to Boston. "I had heard of Joseph DeCamp as a great teacher," she wrote, "so I entered the Cowles Art School, where he was the instructor in life drawing."[16] DeCamp was one of the "Ten American Painters," a group whose common bond was aestheticism executed in a modified style of European impressionism. DeCamp gave up teaching soon after De Cora's arrival, so De Cora enrolled in Boston's School of the Museum of Fine Arts to study with Frank Benson, also one of the "Ten," and Edmund C. Tarbell, leader of the Boston School. She also took at least one decoration course, where she made greeting cards with art nouveau lettering.

During this period she contributed a painting for the frontispiece of Francis La Flesche's *The Middle Five: Indian Boys at School* (1900), about his boyhood at an Omaha boarding school. Following this she created several illustrations for *Old Indian Legends* (1901) by Gertrude Bonnin (aka Zitkála-Šá), as well as illustrations of several dozen headpieces and decorative chapter initials for Mary Catherine Judd's *Wigwam Stories* (1901). De Cora designed the covers for all three books in an arts and crafts style using abstract Indian motifs—bows and arrows, teepees, animal horns, and a thunderbird—with complementary lettering. As she told La Flesche, she was not as happy with her illustration work as she was with his book cover.

In 1902, De Cora moved to New York City, where the art scene was less provincial. By the spring of 1905, she was busy with the American ethnomusicologist Natalie Curtis's *The Indians' Book* (1907), a compilation of art, songs, and stories from eighteen tribal nations. Initially, De Cora was hired to create a Ho-Chunk artwork for the Winnebago chapter, but she ended up rendering original lettering to complement art made by specific tribal artists for each of the book's eighteen chapter heads.

Curtis's recollections reveal De Cora's early role introducing and popularizing Native design: "I asked Angel De Cora to make a design for the title-page of her own tribe, the Winnebago people. When she brought me the finished page, it bore, in addition to the design, the legend, 'Lake Indians—Winnebago,' in letters so beautiful and of such startling originality that my publishers declared: 'We can't have one page looking like this and the others labeled with prosaic printing! We must have this sort of lettering all through the book.'"[17] The publisher's designer further exclaimed that De Cora's "structural ideas for decorative forms," were "unlike anything that's ever been done with the alphabet before." She "invented a different kind of lettering for every Indian picture, and the forms of the letters were composed of *motifs* from the drawings which they accompanied."[18] For example, one chapter's lettering cleverly reflects the pictograph of a Plains ledger artist.[19] De Cora's work for *The Indians' Book* shows her early role in introducing and popularizing Native design, refuting John Ewers's dismissal of her Indianness. Curtis claimed that although De Cora "started her career by illustrating books of Indian tales," she "later looked down upon these early efforts, for her greatest work lay in decorative design."[20]

De Cora was educated when reformers promoted either the complete assimilation of Native children or returned them as cultural missionaries to their reservations. Yet she helped in some measure to transform this White supremacist attitude for the next generation after the Commissioner of Indian Affairs appointed her in 1906 to establish the innovative "Native Indian Art" Department at Carlisle Indian Industrial School in Pennsylvania. She instructed students in the design of book covers, lettering, and head- and tailpieces, but her curriculum mostly emphasized the design of more salable items: "We can perpetuate the use of Indian designs by applying them on modern articles of use and ornament that the Indian is taught to make," she said. "I ask my pupils to make a design for a frieze for wall decoration, also borders for printing, designs for embroidery of all kinds, for wood-carving and pyrography, and designs for rugs."[21]

In the fall of 1907, De Cora presented a paper at the National Educational Association Conference to inform fellow educators about her first year of teaching. Her presentation challenged their primitivist perception of what counted as art and, more importantly, who counted as an artist:

In exhibitions of Indian school work, generally, the only traces of Indian one sees are some of the signatures denoting clannish names. In looking over my pupil's native design work, I cannot help calling to mind the Indian woman, untaught and unhampered by the white man's ideas of art, making beautiful and intricate designs on her pottery, baskets and beaded articles, which show the inborn talent. She sits in the open, drawing her inspiration from the broad aspects of Nature. Her zigzag line indicates the line of the hills in the distance, and the blue and white background so usual in the Indian color scheme denotes the sky. Her bold touches of green, red and yellow she has learned from Nature's own use of those colors in the green grass and flowers, and the soft tones that were the general tone of the ground color in the days of skin garments, are to her as the parched grass and the desert. She makes her strong color contrasts under the glare of the sun, whose brilliancy makes even her bright tones seem softened into tints. This scheme of color has been called barbaric and crude, but then one must remember that in the days when the Indian woman made all her own color, mostly of vegetable dyes, she couldn't produce any of the strong, glaring colors they now get in aniline dyes.[22]

Opening page of "Dakota" from *The Indians' Book*, compiled by Natalie Curtis, 1907. The lettering is by Angel De Cora (Hinook Mahiwi Kilinaka). The image of a Dakota brave and medicine man is by Tatanka-Ptecila (Short Bull), a Dakota Indian. The warrior's horned headdress represents "divine power, the insignia of the Holy Man or Man of Medicine," as noted in the text.

De Cora's essential observations are still taught today in Native art classes, but without attribution to her. Yet she was a key figure in America's arts and crafts movement, as one of the few to infuse it with insider knowledge about the esoteric elements of Native design. As a female in a male-dominated culture of professionalism, she popularized knowledge about Native art and design, hoping that the dissemination of authenticity would revive the pride and economic viability of

"Away with Your White Man's Art!" *Detroit Free Press,* **July 28, 1907. The headline misidentifies Angel De Cora as "Sioux."**

Native Americans who were (and still are) historically traumatized by Indian removals, assimilation policies, and cultural genocide.

In 1911, De Cora helped found the Society of American Indians, a pan-Indian progressive group dedicated to uplifting Native peoples. During the SAI's first conference, she gave a presentation, stating, "Manufacturers are now employing Indian designs in deteriorated forms. If this system of decoration was better understood by the designers how much more popular their products would be in the general market."[23] She believed her Carlisle students were primed for this role, but she also stressed that Native women could obtain more financial independence for their families by applying their tribal designs to popular items.

Eventually, De Cora hoped to quit the bureaucratic Indian Service that administered Carlisle and other Indian schools to collaborate with her husband, William "Lone Star" Dietz, a Carlisle football player who assisted her in the Carlisle art department.[24] They worked together on Carlisle's innovative monthly arts and crafts style magazine, which became a model for those of all Indian schools. They also co-illustrated Elaine Goodale Eastman's *Yellow Star: A Story of East and West* (1911) and Ruth Everett Beck's *The Little Buffalo Robe* (1914), but De Cora did most of the work and her dream of collaborating meaningfully with Dietz was unfulfilled. Dietz left Carlisle to coach college football in 1915, and the couple divorced in November 1918.[25] De Cora died three months later on February 19, 1919, a victim of the flu pandemic.

"Angel always insisted that she had no more talent than any other Indian woman, because they had been natural crafts people and artists from prehistoric times," wrote Natalie Curtis. "'The only difference between me and the women on the reservations,'" De Cora had told her, "'is that I have chosen to apply my native Indian gift in the white man's world.'" Unfortunately, as Curtis rued after her death, "there is little tangible evidence that now can be shown of what Angel wrought, and above all, of what she dreamed."[26] But what De Cora became inspired a generation of Native people to remember their history, honor their culture, and continue designing and creating beautiful art pieces that both reflect—and challenge—the notion of authenticity.

INTRODUCING
ANIMISM

EUGENE A. NIDA
WILLIAM A. SMALLEY

A Black Renaissance Woman: Louise E. Jefferson

Tasheka Arceneaux-Sutton

There aren't that many well-known Black women graphic designers, not many at all. Perhaps some graphic designers have heard of Gail Anderson, Cheryl D. Miller, and the late Sylvia Harris. Despite these great women and their accomplishments, only Anderson is mentioned in any significant graphic design history, and she is included only in a caption in *Meggs' History of Graphic Design*, for the first time in the sixth edition. None of them is mentioned in a history's text. Nor is the cartographer, calligrapher, graphic designer, illustrator, and photographer Louise E. Jefferson.

I first learned of Jefferson while doing research about Black publications at the Amistad Research Center at Tulane University and asked a staff member if he knew of any other Black designers. He said yes and shared with me a short biography about Jefferson and asked if I was interested in any of her work. I was shocked and excited when the he showed me the list of boxes of Jefferson's work that the center had acquired. The center has her entire art estate. At the time, I didn't know much about Black

Louise E. Jefferson, cover of *Introducing Animism*, Eugene A. Nida and William A. Smalley, pamphlet published by Friendship Press, 1959.

23

women in design. I could not believe that I had gone through my whole undergraduate and graduate education without hearing even a mention of Jefferson. I was overwhelmed when I dove into her archive and discovered how much she contributed to the art and design professions.

Louise E. Jefferson was born in 1908 in Washington, DC—the only child of Paul and Louise Jefferson. She came from a long line of musicians. Her mother earned money playing piano and singing on cruise ships on the Potomac River. Both of her parents were pianists, her grandmother was a notable soprano, and her grandfather was an organist at a church in DC. Early on, Jefferson was encouraged to study music, but she decided she wanted a career in visual arts.[1]

Jefferson attended public school in DC, followed by Howard University. She also took private lessons in fine and commercial art and learned calligraphy from her father, who encouraged her as a kid to draw. At an early age, she received advice from her parents to "learn more than one thing well—learn many things."[2] It is evident from all the many talents and skills she acquired that Jefferson heeded her parents' advice. Jefferson once said, "Everything dovetails, you know. You have no idea how many kinds of information, picked up one place or another, will come in handy. A commercial artist must have an encyclopedic mind—for you can never tell what you will be called upon to depict or interpret."[3]

In the mid-1930s, during the Great Depression, Jefferson moved to New York City. It isn't apparent exactly why she moved there, but she called that time "peripatetic, collecting of learning."[4] One reason she went was to see if she could make a career as a photographer and illustrator. "I went to spend ten days," she recalled laughingly in a 1984 interview. "I had just bought what I knew was the most beautiful raccoon coat in the world….I put all the money I had in that pocket. Now, this particular day—it's in February, now—I decided to visit [activist and writer] Pauli [Murray, her college roommate and friend] to see what she was writing, and I'm in the street, showing off…[my] leather jacket and about 45 cents in my pocket. I left the raccoon coat home with all the paper money in it." When she returned to her room to get some books for Murray, she found both coat and money gone. "I never went back home to live. I couldn't face the family."[5] Whatever her reason, she never lived in DC again.

While in New York, Jefferson continued her education at the School of Fine Arts at Hunter College. She studied design and art

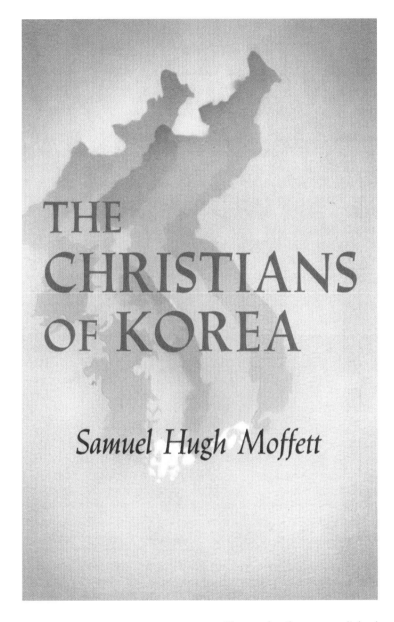

THE
CHRISTIANS
OF KOREA

Samuel Hugh Moffett

Louise E. Jefferson, cover of *The Christians of Korea*, Samuel Hugh Moffett, published by Friendship Press, 1962. composition under the accomplished etcher Ralph Pearson and lithography under the printmaker Riva Helford,

whose social realist work had a considerable influence on her drawings.
The social realism style is evident in
the drawings that Jefferson produced

**Louise E. Jefferson, program for "Jazz
Carousel," the National Urban League
Guild's Beaux Arts Ball, February 1966.**

during her many trips to Africa. From Hunter College, Louise moved
on to study graphic arts and printmaking at Columbia University.[6]

In Manhattan, Louise became friends with several artists and
writers of the Harlem Renaissance. She was one of the founding
members of the Harlem Artists Guild, a program sponsored by

Louise E. Jefferson, program for "Do Your Own Thing!" the National Urban League Guild's Beaux Arts Ball, February 1971.

the Works Progress Administration (WPA).[7] The Harlem Artists Guild's constitution stated: "We, the artists of Harlem, being aware of the need to collaborate in the solution of the cultural, economic, social and professional problems that confront us, do hereby constitute ourselves an organization that shall be known as the Harlem Artists Guild." Other members of the guild included Augusta Savage, Aaron Douglas, Gwendolyn Brooks, and Jacob Lawrence.[8]

Like most young artists, Jefferson struggled financially when she first moved to New York City. She and Murray had a difficult time paying their rent. To make ends meet, Jefferson began to do freelance work designing posters for the Young Women's Christian Association (YWCA). Around the same time, she started doing freelance work for Friendship Press, the National Council of Churches' publishing house, which eventually turned into a full-time job. Friendship Press began publishing books in 1935, making Louise one of the first designers to work there. In 1942, she became the press's art director, and she remained at the company for the next twenty years.[9] Jefferson was the first Black art director in the American publishing industry and perhaps the first woman to hold such a position. Most of her book cover designs (Jefferson illustrated and designed hundreds of books) for Friendship Press included calligraphic and old-style serifs and scripts.

Louise E. Jefferson, NAACP holiday seal: "Seasons Greetings: We Must Still Invest in Freedom," year unknown.

Jefferson's full-time work allowed her to take on many freelance jobs for other New York publishing houses, including Doubleday, Macmillan, and Viking, and for the African American Institute. She also did all the calligraphy work for Columbia University. Jefferson's work covers a wide range, from matchbook covers to book design. In 1937, she received a commission to design sixty posters for the Texas Centennial Exposition for the WPA.

Jefferson never complained about her status as a Black woman in the graphic design industry. She didn't feel that being a Black woman prevented her from doing the work she loved or advancing in her profession. Although racism did not hold her back, her illustrations for *We Sing America*, a 1936 songbook depicting Black and

White children playing together, was the bane of Georgia governor Eugene Talmadge. He ordered the book to be banned and burned.[10]

Besides designing and illustrating many, many books, Jefferson created numerous political and cultural maps and pictograms for the university presses of Oxford, Rutgers, Syracuse, and Columbia. The pictorial map *Twentieth Century Americans of Negro Lineage* is one of her most brilliant personal achievements. She conceived its idea and was responsible for the research, design, and execution of the drawings. The map includes photographs of prominent African Americans, taken by Jefferson herself. Her map *Uprooted People of the U.S.A.* is also groundbreaking. It was the first map to focus on the social costs and impact of the Second World War; most pictorial maps of its period appealed to patriotic sentiments to bolster morale.[11] Themes of dislocation and disruption were common in Jefferson's pictorial maps.

Jefferson designed covers for *The Crisis*, the magazine of the National Association for the Advancement of Colored People (NAACP), and *Opportunity* magazine, associated with the Harlem Renaissance. For forty years, she created all of the NAACP holiday seals, and for twenty years the program covers for the National Urban League's Beaux Arts Ball.[12] Her designs for these two organizations are examples of her calligraphy and lettering skills, which were often combined with old-style serif and script typefaces and the occasional appearance of sans serif and ornamental display typefaces such as Davida and circus fonts with Tuscan serifs. The imagery for the NAACP seals was mainly composed using paper cutouts that create flat areas of color—a style that was very different from the more realistic drawings in her book *The Decorative Arts of Africa.*

Jefferson generated so much work and made contributions to so many areas of art and design that it is sometimes difficult to pin down her style. Nonetheless, the influence and training in calligraphy that she got from her father was significant. Jefferson offered calligraphy and lettering services as a part of her design practice, and there are traces of her techniques in all of her design work. Her style is closest to an italic hand or Chancery style. Her work was so precise that it was often difficult to tell whether her designs included her calligraphy or an actual typeface.

Jefferson's interest in graphic design extended to photography, although she never considered herself a photographer. She complained, "I wish people would stop calling me a photographer."[13] Regardless of her resistance to the title, she carried a camera everywhere. She took well over five thousand photographs, including of many famous and celebrated Black people, among them Martin Luther King Jr., her friend Lena Horne, and her neighbor Thurgood Marshall.[14]

In 1960, Jefferson retired from Friendship Press. Although she said that she never could recall any instances where her skin color was an obstacle in her professional career, she admitted to having had her share of troubles with male superiors. Jefferson retired when she noticed a series of women executives being terminated; she exited before "they got to her."

Over the next ten years, she took a series of five trips to Africa. The first one was for pleasure and became the instigator of the others. One of the trips was supported by a grant from the Ford Foundation; another she undertook as a delegate to the Africa-American Institute's Central African Art Conference. These trips were the background for her book *The Decorative Arts of Africa*, published in 1973. She created almost all of its three hundred photos and drawings of African tribal costumes, decorative designs, and weaponry.[15]

Jefferson received a lot of recognition and awards during her lifetime, but she did not talk readily about her accomplishments. She preferred to talk about her rose garden, her woodworking and metalworking expertise, her calligraphy, her library, her interest in paper-making, or her complete set of commemorative stamps with Black subjects. She was an avid record keeper; in her meticulously organized home, she maintained an extensive chronicle of her long and productive career. In her planner, she kept an account of the weather, making notes on the temperature and whether it was sunny, rainy, or partly cloudy every single day.

Jefferson was also a sports enthusiast, especially for tennis and swimming. Her love for sports reflected her determination to overcome a childhood disability, infantile physical paralysis. Her friend Pauli Murray characterized her as "one of the most agile persons I ever knew."[16] In her younger years, she taught swimming at the YWCA and held an Amateur Athletic Union sprint record in swimming. She filled several summer assignments as a waterfront and crafts counselor at a YWCA camp, and for several years she put her ideas to work at the Publicity and Promotions Department of the New York headquarters of the YWCA.

Beginning in 1951, Jefferson maintained a home near East Litchfield, Connecticut. After she retired from Friendship Press in the early 1960s, Jefferson began living there year-round and set

THE DECORATIVE ARTS OF AFRICA

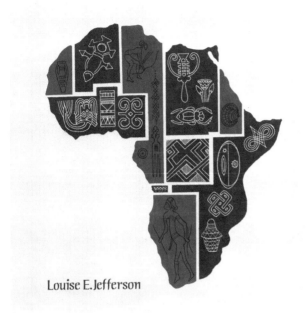

Louise E. Jefferson

Louise E. Jefferson, cover for
Decorative Arts of Africa, **1974.**

up a studio in her home. She lived at the end of a long stretch of dirt road in the countryside, surrounded by nature's sights and sounds. Jefferson was a slender and hardy woman of medium height, often seen with her hair pulled back. A lively and exciting person, she continued to manifest physical energy; people who observed her later in life felt that her "retirement" activities were much like the full-time work of other people. Jefferson never felt that she had any advice to give to young creatives, but she once stated, "I love making paper, I love research, I love writing and photography, in short every aspect of my work pleases me." She continued, "I'm never bored. If anything, I have too many ideas."

WINTER SPORTS

NATIONAL &
STATE PARKS

Women of the Federal Art Project Poster Division

Katie Krcmarik

The Federal Art Project (FAP), originally named Federal One, began in 1935 as an outgrowth of the College Art Association's efforts to help artists struggling during the Great Depression. First Lady Eleanor Roosevelt provided instrumental support to FAP by urging her husband to extend New Deal benefits to the arts; she continued to support the funding even after critics looked to eliminate it as a waste of money. When he took office, President Franklin D. Roosevelt aimed to provide a new deal for everyone, including women, African Americans, and other marginalized groups.[1] The FAP attempted to live up to this mission but often failed to meet these lofty goals. As in other relief efforts, men—typically White men—received benefits before women, based on the men's assumed need to support families and skepticism toward women reporting that they served as the head of their household, in the case of single or widowed mothers.[2] There were also widespread pay discrepancies between White men and both women and people of color at the FAP.[3]

However, the FAP offered opportunities to women and minorities that

Dorothy Waugh, *Winter Sports / National & State Parks*, ca. 1930–40, poster.

33

they might not otherwise have received. Women including Audrey McMahon, Increase Robinson, Florence Kerr, Juliana Force, Augusta Savage, Gwendolyn Bennett, and Ellen S. Woodward held numerous FAP leadership positions at the state, regional, and national levels. Woodward played the most significant role as director of the Women's Division of the Federal Emergency Relief Administration (FERA) and director of the Women's and Professional Projects of the Works Progress Administration (WPA). Additionally, women played significant roles in producing work in all divisions of the project.

As one of the many artistic outlets supported by the FAP, the poster division allowed those formerly employed in roles like art director to find gainful employment. The division produced two million silk-screen copies of thirty-five thousand original poster designs during its operation, before being converted into an arm of the World War II propaganda efforts.[4] The poster division arguably chose the medium of screen printing not just to produce large numbers of high-quality prints but also because of the democratic nature of the medium.[5] Screen printing lent itself well to the very heart of the division's subject matter: health issues and the promotion of states, tourism destinations, and even events produced by the divisions of the FAP. The poster division represented one of the first cohesive efforts to use design, specifically posters, to educate the public about social issues and to deliver health information to the masses.

Artists such as Dorothy Waugh, Charlotte Angus, Mildred Waltrip, and Katherine Milhous used their training in the arts and previous professional experience to leave a significant design legacy. All four of these women worked at a time when the design profession was still in its infancy and women mostly existed in production roles. Most graphic design work involved hand illustration of both images and type, as was the case with the work they produced for the FAP. All four women had demonstrated deft skills as illustrators and artists working in advertising and newspapers and for the National Park Service (NPS) before joining the FAP. The project allowed them to continue growing their skills and in some cases even led to their future careers.

Dorothy Waugh
Dorothy Waugh created several iconic posters for the Federal Art Project's poster division. Her work focused on promoting the national parks. Waugh first became involved with the NPS in 1934.

Dorothy Waugh, *Mystery Veils the Desert / National Parks*, ca. 1930–40, poster.

Her father, Frank Waugh, was a professor of landscape gardening at Massachusetts Agricultural College and a mentor to Conrad Wirth, who spearheaded the project for the Civilian Conservation Corps. Dorothy Waugh compiled the *Portfolio of Comfort Stations and Privies* and *Portfolio of Park Structures* as part of an effort to train new designers to create park structures in harmony with their sites. She presented examples in simple dimensioned drawings assembled in a loose-leaf binder so that new examples could continually be added to the collection.[6] The project ended when the park service decided to pursue a different method for training designers.

Even though this project was discontinued, Wirth continued to work with Waugh on posters promoting recreational activities, including winter sports, in national and state parks as part of the FAP's efforts to promote these national resources. Waugh supervised the posters' production, wrote the copy, and designed the layouts and illustration.[7] The posters' distinct typography and illustrations focused on activities within the park. They remain iconic and earned Waugh mention in an article celebrating the NPS's centennial, where the author noted, "The custom lettering in many of Waugh's posters contain unexpected and sometimes quirky anomalies."[8]

Waugh's lettering alone distinguishes her from others who created posters for the NPS. While most artists chose the sans serif fonts popular during the period, Waugh drew playful, unique letterforms to celebrate qualities specific to the park or activity represented. For example, the type of *Winter Sports / National & State Parks* features italicized letterforms that mimic a person skiing down the slopes. Additionally, Waugh's posters feature illustrations highlighting unique elements from each park or activities within the park. Several of her posters show the direct influence of European modernism, which gained popularity with American designers during the 1930s. Waugh contributed her quirky twists and superior lettering skills to producing posters that helped promote and excite the public about the national parks.

Charlotte Angus, *Air Raid Precautions*, ca. 1941–43, poster.

Beyond this contribution to the NPS and its poster division, Waugh had a long and varied career. She received her education at the Art Institute of Chicago, studying drawing, lettering, design, painting, and typography.[9] (The impact of these studies on her lettering and illustration for the NPS posters is clear.) After graduating, she worked at a commercial art studio in Chicago for three years.[10] She then moved to New York and went to work in the children's book department at Alfred A. Knopf. After the FAP's poster division disbanded, Waugh wrote and illustrated several books about various scientific topics for children in the 1940s and '50s. From 1941 through 1943, she served as a special lecturer and critic in lettering and typography at the New York School of Fine and Applied Art, later Parsons School of Design and now the New School.[11] She also held a publicity position at the Montclair, New Jersey, library, where she coordinated several exhibitions, including a notable one on children's books. As Robert L. Leslie stated in *A-D* magazine, "If taste, high purpose, and skill add up to anything in the graphic arts—and they most certainly do—Dorothy Waugh should be considered one of our best people."[12] Despite her colleagues' esteem and the reputation of her work for the Federal Art Project, little of Waugh's graphic designs beyond these posters is known today.

Charlotte Angus

Charlotte Angus produced work for several branches of the Federal Art Project. Angus started her life in Kansas City, Missouri. After moving to Philadelphia, she studied at the University of the Arts and took lessons at the Graphic Sketch Club. After school, she worked briefly for an advertising agency until she lost the job during the Great Depression.[13] She joined the FAP in 1936, painting sets for the Federal Theater Project. Later, she contributed to the FAP project the Index of American Design and created posters for the poster division. Her designs for the index can be viewed as part of the National Gallery of Art's collection and include drawings for various historical objects, from dishes to quilts. In 1942, as war efforts absorbed the FAP, Angus studied drafting and became a draftswoman for the Naval Air Medical Center in Philadelphia until marrying John Stefanek in 1947.[14] She continued to exhibit her art after settling in southwestern Pennsylvania with her husband.

Charlotte Angus's posters for the WPA feature bold typography and bright colors. Her *Don't Be a Drip! Be Patriotic…Stop Leaks… Save Water* features a simple illustration of a dripping faucet. The red and blue color scheme connects to the poster's patriotic plea. Angus chose a geometric sans serif font, a style that gained popularity in the late 1920s and into the 1930s. The combination of the graphic elements and typography creates a bold but straightforward message. In contrast, her *Air Raid Precautions* relies heavily on typography. The poster features a bright blue background with orange, yellow, and white pops to grab the viewer. Angus uses a hand-drawn display font for the main headline and a geometric sans serif for the remainder of the type. Her bold approach to poster design made wartime messages accessible to a broad audience.

Mildred Waltrip

Mildred Waltrip worked as both a mural painter and a graphic designer for the poster division during her time with the Federal Art Project. Waltrip studied at the Art Institute of Chicago from 1926 to 1933. After completing her education there, she traveled to Paris, where she studied with Fernand Léger. Before joining the FAP, she worked for the advertising department of Marshall Field's from 1936 to 1937, where she illustrated books on topics such as "How to Buy Intelligently."[15] After leaving the FAP, she worked as a commercial artist and illustrated numerous children's science books, including George Barr's Young Scientist series from the 1960s and '70s.

Waltrip's time with the FAP served as the start of her prolific career as a muralist. Creating murals, however, involved challenges for Waltrip; she required special scaffolding when working, due to leg braces she wore after contracting polio.[16] She created several works while working for the mural division, including one featuring episodes from Robin Hood and another depicting the history of aviation. Unfortunately, few still exist, either because the building the mural resided in was destroyed, or the mural was removed following controversy. Her mural *The Process*, in an Oak Park, Illinois, public school, incited rancor in 1995 for its racist depictions of Africans. A proposal called for preserving the art while using lesson plans to acknowledge its problematic nature, but the school board eventually voted to remove two of the mural's panels.[17]

Her design work for the FAP focused on creating promotional posters for art exhibitions and attractions such as the Brookfield Zoo. *Brookfield Zoo Information* features two hippopotamuses layered over a map of the African continent, speaking to the origins of the animal, and a bright green background. She chose an elongated sans serif font; the lettering of "Brookfield Zoo" features a black drop shadow to attract attention. Her poster to promote the Art Institute of Chicago's 49th Annual Exhibition of American Paintings and Sculpture displays a patriotic focus, with stars and stripes serving as a background for an image of a farm and a factory. The Federal Art Project favored such imagery, as celebrating rural and urban American life during that era. She again selected a sans serif font for

Mildred Waltrip, *Information / Brookfield Zoo*, ca. 1936–38, poster.

the type. Both posters layer imagery to create a complex message.

Katherine Milhous

Katherine Milhous created some of the most distinctive posters produced by the Federal Art Project, and she served as a supervisor

FEDERAL ART PROJECT W. P. A. PENNSYLVANIA

Katherine Milhous, *Rural Pennsylvania*, ca. 1936–40, poster.

for the Philadelphia FAP from 1935 to 1940. Milhous was born in Philadelphia to a Quaker family involved in printing. She spent her early years in her father's shop, which initiated her lifetime love of art. Her love of books came from her access to her family's small library.[18] Before her time with the

FAP, Milhous studied at the Pennsylvania Museum and School of Industrial Art and the Pennsylvania Academy of the Fine Arts. She also received scholarships to attend various other art programs, including the Cresson Traveling Scholarship, which allowed her to study abroad in Italy and France. To save money for her artistic adventures, Milhous did drawings commissioned by newspapers at night.[19] After her time with the FAP, she began illustrating children's books. Her book *The Egg Tree*, about a family who painted eggs and hung them on a tree, was selected by the Children's Committee of the AIGA as one of the best-designed books after 1945; it received the Caldecott Medal in 1951.[20] Katherine Milhous spent her life creating spectacular illustrations and sharing her passion for art with children.

Milhous's work for the FAP focused primarily on promoting the state of Pennsylvania. Her works highlight the traditions of the state while enticing viewers to discover its history for themselves. The posters express her deep love for her birthplace and often depict Pennsylvania Dutch people—typically wearing traditional clothing—and symbols common to Amish culture. They feature mainly primary colors, sometimes accented with secondary colors, and they predominantly use sans serif fonts, while using a modern serif or a display font for the word *Pennsylvania*.

More of Milhous's posters exist than from most other female artists of the FAP poster division. While Waugh's work from her time with the FAP is better known, Milhous is perhaps the best-known woman from the poster division because of her extensive career and the accolades she earned after leaving the FAP. Milhous's posters led directly to her career as a book illustrator.[21]

The Legacy of the FAP
The New Deal, including the FAP, sought to bring equity to everyone in the country, including women. It never quite achieved the admirable aspirations set forth by Roosevelt. Still, it did provide opportunities for women like Dorothy Waugh, Charlotte Angus, Mildred Waltrip, and Katherine Milhous to continue their artistic pursuits. It also provided the opportunity for women to take on leadership roles within the project. Their designs testify to their legacy, preserved in permanent collections along with the small number of other posters that survived from the project.

THE FATE OF MEDIEVAL ART IN THE RENAISSANCE & REFORMATION

G.G.COULTON

PART II OF ART AND THE REFORMATION

HARPER TORCHBOOKS /TB 26

One for the Books: Ellen Raskin's Design, Lettering, and Illustration

Briar Levit

I came to the work of Ellen Raskin in a more roundabout way than those who fell in love with her young-adult mystery books as a child or teen. In fact, I wasn't even aware of my initial encounter with her work until I participated in the #BookCover2019 Twitter hashtag that challenged designers to post seven of their favorite book covers over seven days, tagging others to do the same. I'm often paralyzed by indecision at such moments, but the first book I posted was an easy choice: I'd bought it at Goodwill years before, expressly because of its cover, and had displayed it prominently since.

Published in 1958, the book is G. G. Coulton's *The Fate of Medieval Art in the Renaissance and Reformation*. The cover features a bold, abstract woodcut of a medieval cathedral, white against a field of black, with the display type hand cut in a sort of modernist interpretation of uncials and tucked neatly into the negative space of the church's spire.[1] The illustration seemed made for the type. I admit, I have a thing for modernist takes on medieval typography and

Ellen Raskin, cover of *The Fate of Medieval Art on the Renaissance and Reformation*, G. G. Coulton, 1958. Raskin's lettering was often made specifically to complement an illustration.

subjects, but every element on this cover is beautiful, textured, and completely clear and unified. Before this Twitter challenge, I'd never looked to see whether the designer was credited. She was. It was Ellen Raskin.

I tend to get perhaps inordinately excited whenever I see a woman's name listed in the design credits of older works—a small release of the repressed enthusiasm that has bottled up over the years I've studied the disproportionately White, male history of graphic design. And because there is a too-common story of women in the first half of the twentieth century—dropping out of the field or leaving a small body of work due to a world that didn't support working women[2]—I wasn't prepared for the sheer volume and breadth of work I'd find when I started seriously investigating Ellen Raskin. I was equally surprised to find that Raskin was revered and honored in her lifetime: her best-known book, 1978's *The Westing Game*, made her something of a children's-publishing celebrity.

Going Commercial

Raskin graduated from the University of Wisconsin in 1949 with a degree in fine arts, but after three years in New York City, meeting with other woodcut artists in an atelier, she didn't feel that she could actually make a living at being an artist. She got a job at a small ad agency, where she learned the production processes necessary to prepare commercial art for print. From there, she moved on to a slightly bigger agency where she learned how to order type and refined her skills with paste-up mechanicals—still doing production rather than more creative work.[3] It was only at home that she kept her creative self in practice. She purchased a small press to experiment with, later noting that it was "the only way to really learn type."[4]

Once she felt secure in her commercial skills, Raskin quit her studio job to seek freelance projects. She had $200 in the bank, but soon after sending promotional calendars that she designed and printed to art directors and spending an entire day meeting with them, she had a full schedule. She had signed on to $1,000 worth of commercial art contracts for three book jackets and two album covers. From then on, Raskin never had trouble getting work: she went on to design more than one thousand book covers, in addition to advertisements, editorial illustrations, record covers, television telops (TV title cards), and posters.[5]

Raskin's singular focus on financial stability was likely rooted in her experience growing up during the Great Depression.[6] While her family didn't suffer greatly, they did experience a brief period of poverty that seems to have left an indelible mark on her, driving her preoccupation with security. So when Raskin said she stopped making work for pleasure after college, it's very possible she felt there was no other choice. In fact, her money-mindedness extended beyond her design and illustration career: Raskin played the stock market regularly and even fielded offers to manage the mutual funds of friends and colleagues. Notably, her book *The Westing Game* is about a comical group of characters trying desperately to make a money grab. Its protagonist, perhaps not coincidentally, is a little girl named Turtle who plays the stock market by proxy through a naive neighbor.

Raskin's ambition is perhaps related to her focus on money. She openly talked about the fact that she had set a goal of winning a Newbery Medal—the American Library Association's highest honor for children's literature. In a 1985 memorial essay, Raskin's close friend and fellow children's author Alice Bach wrote, "Ellen had a compelling need to be the best. We respect and reward this single-mindedness in business executives; we expect it in our athletes; but we are unsettled by it in writers, who are supposed to be plying their craft for artistic fulfillment."[7] Raskin seemed to be able to combine creativity and ambition unabashedly.

Raskin by Design

Throughout Raskin's life, a progression of styles and approaches can be seen in her work. From her modernist and abstracted woodcut covers of the 1950s and '60s to her more delicate, representational book covers in the late 1960s and '70s and finally her bold, cartoonish illustrations for children, Raskin was never tied to one style. She allowed herself to work in visual languages appropriate to her projects, subjects, and audience.

Her ability to both illustrate and design books sets Raskin apart from many of her peers, but, taking it one step further, her sensitivity to typography and lettering make her unique. Type was almost always integral to her work—never an afterthought and often a focal point. As one profile about her stated, "Nothing ever happens accidentally in an Ellen Raskin book: it is intentional and it is there for a reason, including the exact spot where a page breaks or where a graphic element is to appear."[8] At a time when every piece of type had to be ordered from a type shop or rubbed down from a dry-transfer sheet, it's impressive that a self-taught designer with a background in illustration took such great care.

At the start of her career, Raskin drew a lot of her own lettering to accompany her woodcut illustrations. In keeping with the playfulness of mid-century styles, some, like those seen on the cover of a 1955 album of works by Charles-Marie Widor with boldly illustrated organ-playing hands, featured pointy serifs and jaunty, bouncing baselines. Raskin may have taken her lettering furthest on the cover for P. M. Pasinetti's novel *The Smile on the Face of the Lion* (1965), where flared, almost psychedelic letters cling to the muzzle of a boldly carved lion head. Other letterforms she made took on cleaner and more refined forms, either as serifs or scripts.

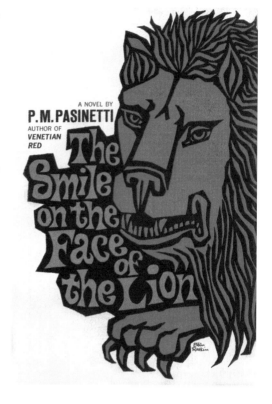

Ellen Raskin, cover of *The Smile on the Face of the Lion*, P. M. Pasinetti, 1965. Raskin used woodcut lettering to make the type of groovy new forms that were popular in the 1960s.

After her first six years of freelance work, Raskin recalled, "I longed to work in a more permanent form—that is, books—and especially to interpret my own ideas for a change, instead of [those of] others." And she did. She wrote, illustrated, and designed twelve picture books and wrote and designed four novels—all while maintaining a freelance practice designing and illustrating for other authors.

"Wordplay, eccentric twists and typographical jokes abound" in the work of Ellen Raskin.[9] As her graphic style evolved to focus more on text, so did her illustrations. Her 1968 children's book *Spectacles* plays with the idea of new ways of seeing the world with poor eyesight. Stippled lettering for the title page kicks off the theme.

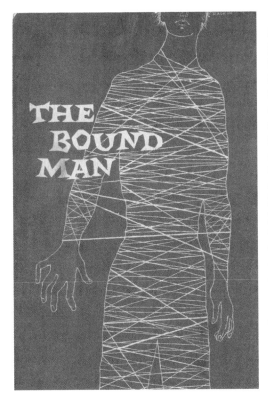

Ellen Raskin, cover of *The Bound Man*, Ilse Aichinger, 1956: another example in which custom lettering complements an illustration by Raskin.

The Mysterious Disappearance of Leon (I Mean Noel) (1971) is filled with wordplay from beginning to end. It was Raskin's first children's chapter book, and when her editor asked what illustrations she had planned for it, she panicked a bit. Raskin was wary of illustrating the characters in a text-based book because she wanted young readers to use their own imaginations; on the other hand, the fact that she was known primarily as an illustrator put added pressure on her decisions. Raskin's solution was to render the bodies of the novel's characters in lettering, with words that reflect their personalities. "The only thing that I could think of to possibly do was to make word pictures, and all those pictures are hand-lettered, made up of hand-lettered words to keep the word image going throughout the book."[10]

In 1974's *Figgs & Phantoms*, Raskin went even further, removing almost all representational illustrative elements to focus on type treatments and handwritten notes and letters. Each chapter also includes an initial cap and an elaborate title treatment.

Sometimes Raskin's lack of a formal education in typography shows: the type she created for the cover of *A & THE, or William T. C. Baumgarten Comes to Town* (1970), for instance, looks heavy handed and awkwardly spaced. But she was clearly looking at typographic trends of the 1960s and '70s. She used new and decorative faces of the period: Bookman Swash for *The Westing Game* and *A Paper Zoo* and heavy slab serifs popular at the time for the covers of *Figgs & Phantoms* and others. In *Twenty-two, Twenty-three* (1976), words, in the form of three-dimensional signage, dominate the cover—a rarity for children's books.

Raskin particularly liked to make eclectic lock-ups of various decorative type-faces that emulated a sort of Victorian/circus style that was popular in the 1960s and '70s. Examples of this include the interior of *Figgs & Phantoms* and the cover of *The World's Greatest Freak Show* (1971). It's important to remember that these lock-ups of typography were not something that could be thrown together and tested with the click of a button. Her roughs and tight sketches for type treatments in *Figgs & Phantoms* show the kind of thought and planning that went into these typographic

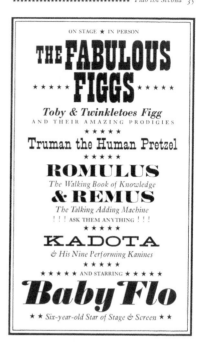

ON STAGE ★ IN PERSON

THE FABULOUS FIGGS

★ ★ ★ ★ ★ ★ ★ ★ ★

Toby & Twinkletoes Figg
AND THEIR AMAZING PRODIGIES
★ ★ ★ ★ ★
Truman the Human Pretzel
★ ★ ★ ★ ★
ROMULUS
The Walking Book of Knowledge
& REMUS
The Talking Adding Machine
! ! ! ASK THEM ANYTHING ! ! !
★ ★ ★ ★ ★
KADOTA
& His Nine Performing Kanines
★ ★ ★ ★ ★
★ ★ ★ ★ ★ AND STARRING ★ ★ ★ ★ ★
Baby Flo
★ ★ *Six-year-old Star of Stage & Screen* ★ ★

Ellen Raskin, typographic illustration from her book *Figgs & Phantoms*, 1974. The type lock-up is designed to move the story forward.

concepts well before the type was ordered, cut, and pasted down for the printer.

Raskin could certainly create elegant or serious type treatments to complement her design and illustration. For books like Gustavus Myers's *History of Bigotry in the United States* (1960 edition), Matthew Josephson's *The Robber Barons* (1962 edition), and August Meier's *Negro Thought in America* (1963 edition), she employed an urgent, heavy sans serif treatment. For books like Henry David Thoreau's *Walden* (1965 edition) and Adrien Stoutenburg and Laura Nelson Baker's *Explorer of the Unconscious: Sigmund Freud* (1965), she used delicate serifs with a literary flavor. She had some go-to approaches, such as combining sharp

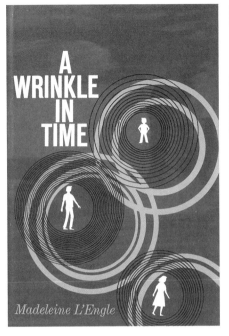

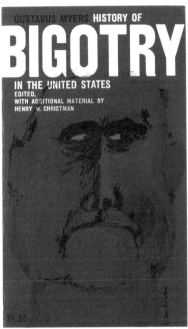

(Left) Ellen Raskin, cover of *A Wrinkle in Time*, Madeleine L'Engle, 1962: one of 1,000 book covers designed by Raskin. (Right) Ellen Raskin, cover of *History of Bigotry in the United States*, Gustavus Myers, 1960. Raskin employs the aggressive quality of large-scale bold grotesque type, contrasted with the portrait of a boorish man with red eyes.

photo type (both sans and serif) with her own roughhewn (often woodcut) illustrations or the aforementioned spikey serifs and mid-century-styled uncials, which she hand cut. Yet she was not hemmed in by any one visual style. In fact, arguably her best-known cover, for Madeleine L'Engle's *A Wrinkle in Time*, uses a sharp grotesque paired with a clean, geometric illustration. This flexibility allowed her to design for many book subjects—poetry, law, fiction, social sciences, mathematics, philosophy, and more.

Raskin took the look of body text as seriously as she did the emotive and display text on her book covers. In a 1983 interview, she noted:

> The printer's galleys come back and they have to be paged.... I think I'm the only writer [to] fortunately have a publisher who allows this—I rewrite for the look of the page. I want my books to look readable. I know that some of the mysteries are

complicated, but [they are] made less so by breaking up the page and by making it look fun to read, fun to hold.[11]

Raskin made similar comments in interviews again and again, noting that such details—the way the type is set, the way it breaks, the size of the book itself—matter in creating books that draw children in and make them want to read the story.

Working Woman

Like many women working outside the home during the women's liberation movement of the 1960s and '70s, Raskin wasn't particularly outspoken about the challenges of women in the illustration and design fields. But her thoughts did creep out from time to time in interviews—perhaps most notably when she was asked about her daily routine and how she balanced a disciplined practice with her responsibilities as a parent. What sociologist Arlie Hochschild termed "the second shift" in her 1989 book of the same name is the expectation that women working outside the home will shoulder the same domestic burdens as those who don't, resulting in a never-ending cycle of work-shop-parent-work-repeat.[12] Around 1950, immediately after graduating from college, Raskin moved to New York City with her first husband and their infant. By the time their daughter was three, they had divorced; it's not clear what Raskin's childcare arrangements were. She described an exhausting workday:

> I would come home, play with [my] daughter. After she was in bed I would stay up and sit down at the drawing board or my printing press and stay there for six hours straight. When I was freelance I would sit down at 9 o'clock in the morning at the drawing board. Not allow myself up until noon. Have a half an hour for lunch, half an hour for shopping for dinner. Sit down again until five and again from 7:30 until 10:00. So this was every day, including Saturday, and it's hard work.

To the specific question of discipline, Raskin continued,

> I have a very crass answer for that and that is [that] I had to make a living, and not only did I have to make a living, I wanted to make a living doing something I not only wanted to do, [but] that I could be good at.[13]

Beyond the systemic issues of the unequal burden of domestic labor, Raskin also faced more overt instances of sexism. "My illustrations are very masculine, which is why I used to sign myself 'E. Raskin,'" she noted in a 1985 interview. "When I was working for Young & Rubicam, the advertising agency, some of their clients wouldn't employ a woman. Easily enough, I became 'E. Raskin.' No one knew any differently."[14]

The characters she developed in *The Westing Game* offer more clues to Raskin's beliefs about gender roles and feminism. Turtle, the book's thirteen-year-old protagonist, is the closest in age to the book's likely readers, and both her intelligence and her status as the weirdest of the Westing children are invitations for readers to sympathize with and relate to her. Her beautiful older sister, Angela, meanwhile, is discounted as nothing more than a pretty face who doesn't need to go to college or even get a driver's license; as the girls' mother puts it, she can get a man to chauffeur her around. Neither sister gets a fair chance to show her worth—the former because she is ignored and the latter because she is repressed by her overbearing, ambiently sexist parents.

Despite the challenges she faced, Raskin carried on with her work successfully, until her untimely death in 1984 at the age of fifty-six, as a result of a connective tissue disease. She lived in tolerant New York City, had a supportive partner in her second husband, and was actively engaged in the publishing world through events and conferences, which certainly helped her as a woman working in what was still predominantly a man's world of design. And while Raskin is still best known for her authorship of children's and young-adult books, I put her forward here as an auteur of word, letter, and image. She took all three and wielded them deftly—with wit, humor, beauty, and style. And though contemporary design is often rightfully critical of the concept of the singular creator,[15] as it focuses on style rather than understanding the context in which the design was created, I would argue that there still aren't enough stories of women as singular designers working in the mid-twentieth century to exclude a career like Raskin's. There is still much to learn from her life and evolution as artist, illustrator, designer, and writer.

For her part, Raskin received repeated recognition throughout her life from the Society of Illustrators, American Institute of Graphic Artists, the Art Directors Club of New York, and even the Type Directors Club. And, perhaps most important, she won that Newbery Medal, just as she said she intended to do.

JANUARY /1975 $1.00

Ms.

**INTERNATIONAL
WOMEN'S YEAR!
BERNADETTE
IN IRELAND...
3 MARIAS OF
PORTUGAL...**

**EROTIC ART IN THE
U.S.... A BLUE-
COLLAR HEROINE
FROM FRANCE
...2 SISTERS
IN GHANA...**

IT'S YOUR YEAR

**PLUS: EPHRON, MILLETT, STEINEM,
STYRON & MUCH MORE**

IND 33105

Bea Feitler: The *Sir* to *Ms.* Years
Tereza Bettinardi

A young, vivacious woman caught in an instant. As she takes off her sunglasses with a broad smile, we can almost hear her bracelets jingling while she moves toward the camera. The figure stands out from twilight against an almost imperceptible background. Thanks to a low wall at the back, the mysterious setting is identified: Rodrigo de Freitas Lagoon, one of the postcard scenes of Rio de Janeiro. It was taken in the 1970s by the Spanish-born Brazilian fashion and celebrity photographer Antonio Guerreiro.

The career of the woman in the picture, Brazilian graphic designer Beatriz Feitler (better known as Bea), was driven by movement. "The closest thing to motion is editorial design," she stated when asked about working in magazines.[1] Feitler's story is like an editorial-design premise brought to life: her fascination with ballet, her move to New York, and her contribution to bringing feminism into the mainstream through her design work in the United States. This essay bridges two distinctive moments in an eleven-year period during Feitler's career, from her first

Bea Feitler, cover of *Ms.* magazine, January 1975. The distorted type and layered elements—including a large silver-foil square—embody a postmodernist aesthetic.

professional experience in Rio de Janeiro at **Bea Feitler in Rio de Janeiro** *Senhor* (Sir) magazine in 1960 to her role in the **during the 1970s.** early '70s as art director of *Ms.*, the first commercial magazine in the United States to become a major chronicle and symbol of the women's movement.

Although Feitler's dazzling career as a graphic designer and art director has been rediscovered in recent years, the current increased enthusiasm for women designers risks missing a true understanding of their accomplishments.[2] The mere attempt to balance the quota of work by women in design reference books with simple mentions does not represent the nuances and singularity of their voices. In fact, a collection of those testimonials is long overdue.

After reading several interviews with Feitler where she talks about her work, I found it embittering to realize that even though she passed away four decades ago, one year before I was even born, I can still relate to most of her professional dilemmas, including the sorrows of negotiating salary increases and graphic design credit, and the lack of women in positions of leadership in the creative industry. I was struck by how many times she talked about her work in terms of opportunities, mentioning the importance for an art director—and, later, a freelancer—of cultivating professional

FERNANDO
SABINO
O
HOMEM
NU

Bea Feitler, cover of *O homem nu*, Fernando Sabino, published by Editora do Autor, 1960. The justified lilac and orange typography became a sort of identity that would be explored on subsequent Sabino book covers.

relationships and discussing her pursuit of financial compensation and authorship.[3]

Bea Feitler was born in Rio de Janeiro on February 5, 1938. As with many of her contemporaries, her childhood was shaped by the aftermath of World War II. Two years before her birth, her parents, Erna and Rudi Feitler, like many German Jews, fled Nazi Germany and settled in Rio's up-and-coming Ipanema neighborhood, where Feitler grew up.

From her teenage years, Feitler showed an interest in art and illustration. With her parents' encouragement and financial support, she moved to New York in 1956 to study at Parsons School of Design. Three years later, she received a degree in graphic arts and advertising and returned to Rio de Janeiro to work as a professional graphic designer.

An unprecedented environment of optimism took over Rio de Janeiro during the 1950s, as it emerged from its colonial past to become a cosmopolitan city of three million inhabitants with a strong cultural identity. New forms of music, cinema, and art arose almost simultaneously—no wonder so many of them expressed novelty in their names: *bossa nova*, *cinema novo*, the neo-concrete movement. Brazil's new capital, Brasilia, was built from scratch over an impressively short five-year span and was inaugurated in early 1960. It was a unique moment of great national self-esteem, which would come to an end in 1964 with Brazil's civil-military coup.

Feitler started her career as assistant designer at *Senhor* in 1960. Despite the publication's short life, it embodied the spirit of Brazilian mod-

ernism—as well as the optimism of bossa nova—like no other magazine. The emerging Brazilian intelligentsia—including prominent authors such as Clarice Lispector, João Guimarães Rosa, and Jorge Amado—published their writings in its pages.[4] *Senhor*'s innovative approach linking graphic design to the visual arts is of great importance in Brazilian graphic design history.[5] The magazine's team of artists and designers included the painter Glauco Rodrigues and the cartoonist Jaguar. Feitler worked under the direction of the artist and designer Carlos Scliar, whom she identified as her "greatest supporter and mentor" at that time.[6] Feitler would remember Scliar as the first person to give her a work opportunity after her graduation, and the two kept in contact throughout the years.[7]

It is difficult to identify the extent of Feitler's contribution to *Senhor* due to the absence of specific credits. Out of a total of fifty-nine published covers, three were properly credited to her. From the extensive literature available in Brazil about the legacy of *Senhor*, one can infer that Feitler was the only female designer working for the magazine.

Carlos Scliar left *Senhor* in 1960, along with almost the whole team, leading to the magazine's closure in January 1964. This small group of artists and designers would meet again through their work designing book covers for Editora do Autor, another innovative yet brief initiative of the Brazilian publishing industry. Founded in 1960 by writers Fernando Sabino and Rubem Braga, the publishing house aimed to increase the usual 10 percent of royalties from book sales to authors. In order to do so, Sabino and Braga relied on their own reputation as well-known writers.

The few covers Feitler designed for Editora do Autor figure among the most brilliant designs of the decade.[8] The cover for Fernando Sabino's *O homem nu* (The nude man) shows Feitler's nascent proficiency in using type and shifts of scale, which would become prominent in her later works. The anthropomorphic use of the word *nu* ("naked") ambiguously shows the words becoming both the design and the message. There's a close relationship between this cover and Tarsila do Amaral's oil painting *Abaporu* (1928). The painting borrows its name from the combination of two words from the language of the Tupi-Guarani Indigenous people: *aba* ("man") and *poru* ("who eats human flesh"). *Abaporu* became the symbol of the early Brazilian modernist movement, which recognized Brazil's colonial trauma and imagined a national modern culture arising from the symbolic digestion—or artistic "cannibalism"—of outside influences. Feitler's book cover, like Amaral's painting, shows a monstrous solitary figure occupying space.

While working for Editora do Autor, Feitler cofounded the design firm Estúdio G in partnership with Jaguar and Glauco Rodrigues, graphic designers she had met at *Senhor*. Their work sprawled from posters for art galleries to visual identities for local retail businesses, but Estúdio G closed in less than six months.[9] Feitler later described the year she spent working in Rio as a twenty-four-year old as frustrating.[10] She highlighted the lack of opportunities for women in Brazil and the poor reception of her work by local clients.

Nevertheless, her short professional experience at *Senhor* was enough to rocket her to an international career. In early 1961, Feitler was back in New York after accepting an assistant designer position on Marvin Israel's team at *Harper's Bazaar*.[11] Israel had been one of her teachers at Parsons and had recently become the magazine's art director. Two years later, when Israel left the magazine, Feitler became its co–art director with Ruth Ansel; both were twenty-five years old at the time. This was a remarkable achievement, even by today's standards.

Undoubtedly, Feitler's decade spent working at *Bazaar* was her coming-of-age period as a graphic designer. Her work there displayed all her skills, especially her ability to combine distinct references: pop culture with ballet, classical cinema with fashion, humor with political activism. She built a reputation for getting what she needed in photographs and not mincing words of criticism to her collaborators. This pursuit of aesthetic integrity and deep respect for artists made it possible for her to nurture an important network of collaborators, from Richard Avedon and Hiro to Bill Silano and Otto Stupakoff.

The output of Feitler and Ansel's ten-year tenure at *Bazaar* is remarkable. These two young women brought to the paste-up desk what they saw on the streets, in many ways renegotiating the commercial representation of women in the 1960s. But inside the offices of the Hearst Corporation, which owned *Bazaar*, changes were very slow. Feitler recalled:

> It was great to work at the magazine; there was freedom to innovate and time to work on concurrent works. However, I wanted to be an art director on my own, to have more freedom and a higher salary, because ours was divided in two, just like work. After 11 years I thought I could demand my share. They didn't like the idea. So I quit.[12]

After leaving *Bazaar* in 1971, Feitler was invited to become the art director of a new magazine, *Ms.*, founded and edited by Gloria Steinem. Its preview issue was launched as a sample insert in *New York* magazine. As *Ms.* turned "a movement into a magazine," Feitler's contributions laid the groundwork that shaped contemporary feminism in the mainstream media.[13]

The first independently published issue of *Ms.* hit the newsstands in 1972. Its cover shows a Godzilla-sized Wonder Woman storming through a city street. Feitler recalled, "When they first brought me the comic strip, I had never heard of her, but I had a feeling it was the right thing to have her as the symbol of the growing movement." She goes on, "You can imagine how delighted I was when readers and then manufacturers agreed upon it, although personally I might add that I didn't like the cover that much."[14]

Compared to Feitler's previous publications, *Ms.* was a wordy magazine. Bold graphics were a great antidote and equalizer. Her talent in connecting and rebuilding images found fertile ground in the pages of *Ms.*, where controversial messages were powerfully

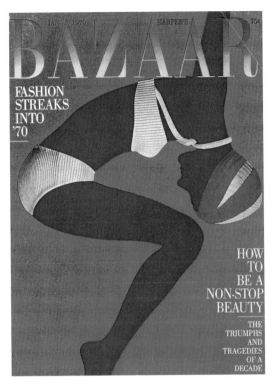

communicated through Feitler's witty designs. An ordinary photograph of a traffic fight in downtown Rio de Janeiro, for instance, became the background for the cover story, "Do Women Make Men Violent?"

In an interview from 1973, published by a Jewish community newspaper in Brazil, Feitler talked about her work at *Ms.* The article's title summarized it: "This Lady Does Not Participate in the American Feminist Movement. But She Works (a Lot) for It."[15] Feitler acknowledged that her ongoing work with the magazine made her more and more feminist. In an interview two years later, she was even clearer:

Bea Feitler, cover of *Harper's Bazaar*, January 1970, photography by Alberto Rizzo. Using both illustration and photography, the Brazilian-born designer often explored the female silhouette in her work.

Any woman who is committed to being an individual is a feminist. Any woman who is intelligent is feminist. Any woman who values herself has to be feminist. I was never involved in the movement. I think I was liberated before any women's lib.[16]

Feitler's role at *Ms.* expanded her practice to include a variety of concurrent projects related to the feminist movement. One remarkable example of this lineage of projects is her design for the book *Wonder Woman*. Remarkable still is her prominent design credit on the title page—an ambition of many designers, but the achievement of few. "I have always been lucky enough to make it a rule, that my name as a designer goes on the title page of every book I've done. Most people don't realize that it is a struggle," Feitler said.[17] Few designers accomplish such an extraordinary feat even today.

In 1976, Feitler left *Ms.* to start her own firm. She had developed a long-term relationship with *Rolling Stone* and had designed numerous books, covers, record sleeves, catalogs, and advertising campaigns for a variety of other clients. She maintained strong collaborations with Brazilian editors and publishing houses, completing important projects for book covers, magazines, and posters. One of these was the video lettering for *Os Doces Bárbaros*, a 1976 documentary film directed by her childhood friend Jom Tob Azulay about the tour celebrating the singers Caetano Veloso, Gilberto Gil, Maria Bethânia, and Gal Costa.[18] Before dying of cancer on April 8, 1982, at age forty-four, Feitler finished a vibrantly post-modern prototype for the first issue of Condé Nast's resurrected *Vanity Fair* magazine.

(Above and opposite) Bea Feitler, typographic covers for *Ms.*, December 1972 and March 1973. The all-type holiday cover proclaiming "Peace on earth, good will to people" is one of Feitler's most remarkable works at *Ms.* By tweaking the deep red and forest green associated with Christmas to Day-Glo hot pink and fluorescent green, she reframed a phrase with foundations in Christianity to capture the emotive resonance surrounding the holiday season.

When recounting all of her accomplishments, it is hard to believe that Feitler's career lasted for only about twenty years. Her career and life, characterized by constant movement, crossed boundaries between what she could take for granted and what was risky and unproven—a path that was easily navigated by her contemporary male colleagues, but not as easily for a woman. As Feitler described it, "When I started, I thought I would have done well as a freelancer,

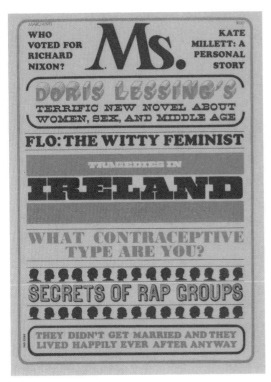

but it felt like I had to have a *job*. I was not psychologically ready, doubly so because I was a woman."[19] Feitler's achievements, in an era when women were expected to express gratitude for the privilege of doing something interesting in order to gain a prominent position in the publishing industry, become even more important, reflecting a pioneering approach.

Graphic design was once called "commercial art"—a term that perhaps fell out of favor because of its built-in contradictions. Feitler dared to choose the best from both scenarios—commerce and art. The joy of doing fueled her single-minded commitment to her craft. There was only work: "Every book I do nurtures my talent, which is really the most important thing to me. No matter what I do, how commercial or aesthetic, it all comes out of my guts."[20]

As a female designer, I often feel like I am running a relay race with no knowledge of what is being passed from one runner to the next. As we fill the gaps of graphic design history, it is still rare to find literature that focuses on what makes women designers' outputs so important. It is our duty to conjure up a sense of the individuals behind the work; by gathering their stories and giving proper space for female graphic designers to share their experiences, we may further their legacy.

By Women, for Women: Suffragist Graphic Design

Meredith James

Women's suffrage in the United States is not marked by a single event or moment in time. The right to vote has been a hard-fought series of accomplishments, by generations of women, with gains granted in stages. The process remains incomplete, as certain groups continue to be disenfranchised even today. Yet, it is hard to deny the impact of the Nineteenth Amendment. First introduced to Congress in 1878, it took until 1919 to pass and 1920 to be ratified. The amendment guarantees women the right to vote. It was a watershed moment that became the foundation upon which all subsequent women's rights efforts have been built.

The fervor and collective energy put into passing a national voting law peaked in the decades leading up to 1920. During this time, women across the country mobilized and organized. Suffragists not only lobbied county, state, and national governments, but also staged parades and vigils. Women's clubs were formed. Suffragists took to writing in newspapers and journals and started their own publications. Women protested. They were harassed, assaulted, and jailed. It was a seismic effort.

Katherine Milhous, *Votes for Women*, 1915, postcard.

(Opposite) Evelyn Rumsey Cary, *Woman Suffrage...*
Give Her of the Fruit of Her Hands..., **1905**, oil painting.
(Above) Bertha M. Boyé, *Votes for Women*, **1911**,
lithographic poster.

The voice of the movement was decentralized and pluralistic. Suffragist women represented diverse regional, economic, educational, and cultural backgrounds. The visual culture of the movement was equally polyvocal. Women used publications, leaflets, postcards, and posters—timely, dominant vehicles of communication—to speak to particular audiences.

The role that print materials played in giving voice to the suffrage movement cannot be overstated. In Southern California, more than three million pieces of literature were distributed in the year leading up to the 1911 statewide measure for suffrage. In the 1915 New York campaign, suffragists distributed almost seven million posters alone.

Of the professional designers who created materials for the suffrage campaign, only a very small number of them are known to be women, and even fewer women of color. It was common at the time for work made by women to be uncredited or for their identities to be subsumed by the imprints of the printing and publishing companies that produced their work.

"If women aren't cited for what they did and what impact they had, they are lost to memory," art historian Jo Lauria stated. It is one thing to catalog the art and design of the women's movement, but it is another thing altogether to showcase work made by women, for women, centered entirely around women's power. Print work made for the suffrage movement holds a special place in our canon—even more so when it was made by women designers, for this work represents the voices of women themselves at a crucial moment in women's history. Below are eight of these notable American women.

Cary's and Boyé's Iconic Posters

Evelyn Rumsey Cary was an artist and art patron from New York. She exhibited her work at the Buffalo Fine Arts Academy and the Buffalo Society of Artists but gained notoriety when a painting of hers was selected for the 1901 Pan-American Exposition, also in Buffalo. Cary's best-known piece, *Woman Suffrage*, originated as an oil painting and dates to ca. 1905. It was a ubiquitous image for the suffrage movement, widely reprinted in a variety of media, including on the back cover of the January 1918 edition of the *Woman Citizen*.

Cary's composition is symmetrical, focusing on a slightly elongated central female figure draped in classical robes. Toward her feet, the draping transforms into tree roots, while the tips of her fingers similarly transform into the branches of a fruit tree. The painting is teal monochrome, framed in gold ink, with the words

The Woman's Era.

VOL. II. NO. 1.   BOSTON, MASS., APRIL, 1895   PRICE 10 CENTS.

JOSEPHINE ST. P. RUFFIN.
(By permission of Boston Journal.)

FLORIDA RUFFIN RIDLEY.

NOTES AND COMMENTS.

Mrs. Abby Morton Diaz gave the first in her series of talks on the "Science of Human Beings" before the Era Club Tuesday evening, March 28, at the Charles St. Church vestry. At a time and in a community where people are talked to, and at, and about until they are more inclined to run from rather than to lectures, it is gratifying to note that, so novel in scheme and so inspiring in result was this talk, that the enthusiasm created by it is likely to run and spread and create a wide interest to hear the remainder of the course. These lectures are given at the Club's expense and are free to the public. The next one will be given April 11.

Mrs. Fannie Barrier Williams, editor of the Illinois department of the WOMAN'S ERA and secretary of the Illinois Woman's Alliance, is expected to deliver a series of lectures in New England in April.

The March literary meeting of the Woman's Era Club was in charge of the Committee on Manners and Morals, Miss Eliza Gardner, chairman.

Two well prepared papers were read, one by Mrs. Agnes Adams on "Our Needs," and the other by Mrs. Alice Casneau on "Morals and Manners." As a result of suggestions made by Mrs. Casneau, the following resolution was adopted by the Club:

WHEREAS, The Woman's Era Club having had their attention called to the very common practice of putting tickets in the hands of children to be sold for the benefit of different objects, do herewith

RESOLVE, That inasmuch as the custom of permitting young girls to solicit men to buy tickets from them is damaging to modesty and a menace to morality, we do set the seal of our condemnation upon it, and call upon the church people especially to help us abolish the custom.

The Club then listened to an interesting narration by its president, who went as a delegate to the Triennial Council of Women at Washington, and then farther south on a visit to Women's clubs in that section. The president reported that she had returned with health and enthusiasm in and for our women burning more brightly than ever. Her stay was short, but long enough to show her that the women of the south-land are as active in trying to "help make the world bet-

Mrs. N. A. Ridley
Nov 26, 1930

Josephine St. Pierre Ruffin, the *Woman's Era* 2, no. 1, April 1895.

Woman Suffrage reversed out and stacked along the left and right edges. The figure is adorned with a wreath that signified the triumph and power that a woman could claim. The figure is clearly feminine, but not sexualized. Emphasis is placed on the intricacy and tonal range of her face and head; it is her ideas and beliefs that are of most importance. The text beneath the figure reads, "Give her of the fruit of her hands, and let her own works praise her in the gates." It is a biblical quote, from Proverbs, a reference that would have been familiar to suffragists. Through the imagery, the message is reinforced: the woman is rooted into the ground, but her labor is abundant and connected to the heavens, adorned in gold.

Bertha M. Boyé grew up in the San Francisco Bay Area and studied at the Mark Hopkins Institute of Art. Her iconic 1911 *Votes for Women* lithograph is considered to be the most widely recognized poster produced during the suffrage movement. It was Boyé's winning entry in a competition sponsored by the College Equal Suffrage League in San Francisco and was used extensively in the successful 1911 campaign to pass suffrage in California. As in Cary's *Women Suffrage*, the central figure is slightly elongated; she is drawn in a symmetrical composition, with an abstracted Bay Area landscape behind her. Her head is surrounded by a sun, acting as a halo, and the bob cut of her hair refers to the idea of the modern woman as she was emerging in the early twentieth century. Boyé's woman inhabits a large majority of the space, pushing edge to edge. In her hands, the figure holds a white banner that reads "Votes for Women."

Boyé's lithograph indicates abstraction in the form. Most of the design is made up of single-color, simplified shapes, from the orange bridge and sun, penciled-in mountains, and colorless water to the yellow expanse of the woman's robes. The figure's physique is again de-emphasized, drawn without feminization or sexualization, and rendered as little more than a loose sketch. The entire piece reads as if the woman is quietly but firmly proclaiming her position. Like Cary's, Boyé's composition does something of note: it emphasizes the woman's face above all else. The widest range of tonality exists from her collarbone up. The work captures and conveys a female sense of self. The only other elements in the composition that carry an equal visual weight are the figure's fingers and the banner she holds in them. In *Votes for Women* Boyé has given highest priority to a twinning of idea and identity.

The Ruffins and Publication Design

One of the dominant means by which African American women documented their experiences during the suffrage movement was through publications. In the early 1890s, the first newspaper established and run entirely by Black women, the *Woman's Era,* was founded by Josephine St. Pierre Ruffin and her daughter, Florida.

COPYRIGHT, 1915, BY NATIONAL WOMAN SUFFRAGE PUBLISHING CO., INC.

Mary Shepard Greene Blumenschein,
***Votes for Women*, 1915, postcard.**

Josephine St. Pierre Ruffin was born in Boston and educated on the East Coast. She was a staunch abolitionist and suffragist, and her interests in activism, journalism, and women's rights coalesced when she published the first edition of the *Woman's Era.* Ruffin was managing editor and handled many of the publication's necessary operations. She also notably designed layouts for the *Woman's Era.* Josephine's daughter, Florida Ruffin Ridley, shared her interests in journalism and activism and worked as her assistant editor.

In the *Woman's Era*, Ruffin created a national, unifying platform for the voices of Black women from various club organizations across the country. "Ruffin's journalistic work enhanced the pride and confidence of thousands of her sisters," notes the cultural historian Rodger Streitmatter. The *Woman's Era* published pro-suffrage information and content—for instance, an homage to suffrage activist Lucy Stone was printed on the front cover of the first edition—but overall the publication was focused more broadly on the advancement of Black women in other aspects of their lives.

Josephine St. Pierre Ruffin, through the *Woman's Era*, was also responsible for putting out a call for a national convention of clubwomen, which occurred in 1895. As a result, Black women's clubs merged, and merged again in 1896. The resulting group, the National Association of Colored Women (NACW), grew to some

Blanche Ames Ames, *The Map Blossoms*, 1915, editorial cartoon.

tens of thousands of women strong by the time the Nineteenth Amendment passed.

Postcards by Milhous and Blumenschein

Katherine Milhous was a well-known children's book author, illustrator, and poster designer. Milhous attended both the Pennsylvania Academy of the Fine Arts and the Pennsylvania Museum and

School of Industrial Art. While in school, she earned scholarships and supported herself as a newspaper illustrator. As a professional, she designed exceptional posters for the Works Progress Administration and worked at *Scribner's* magazine as a staff designer, before embarking on a long career as a children's book illustrator. Her suffrage work dates to when she was a student.

In 1915, Milhous designed a popular pro-suffrage postcard entitled *Votes for Women*. It's a two-color print on glossy card stock, with an aesthetic that is loose and gestural. There are six captioned panels that follow a sequential narrative, asking a prime question of the movement: If it does not "unsex" a woman to work in the home, at a factory, or as a nurse, how could voting possibly "unsex" her? Issues of gender were front and center in the suffrage debate. The question of what makes a woman "womanly" was ever present. Pro-suffrage postcards often had to combat sexist stereotypes put forth by anti-suffrage campaigns. In this postcard, Milhous directly challenges those biases.

Mary Shepard Greene Blumenschein created another pro-suffrage postcard in 1915 that reinforced positive depictions of women. In Blumenschein's postcard, a young suffragist with modern hair and clothes is draped in a golden sash printed with the words *Votes for Women*.

The postcard reflects Blumenschein's background as a painter and book illustrator. She studied at Pratt Institute (where she would later teach) and honed her skills studying in Paris, where her work gained an international audience. Her paintings are exquisite. The pensiveness of the woman she painted in *Un Regard Fugitif* is echoed in the young woman illustrated in the *Votes for Women* postcard. Her style expresses a romantic realism that represents women as feminine and contemplative yet full of vitality.

Ames and Knobe Mapping Victories

In the years surrounding the 1848 Seneca Falls Convention, suffragist and abolitionist causes were heartily connected. But after the Civil War, when the Fourteenth and Fifteenth Amendments excluded women from true citizenship and voting rights, the women's movement was breached. Susan B. Anthony and Elizabeth Cady Stanton refused to support the amendments and formed an all-women group called the National Woman Suffrage Association (NWSA). Lucy Stone and Julia Ward Howe, proponents of universal suffrage, supported the amendments as they were and formed the American Woman Suffrage Association (AWSA).

The NWSA's focus was federal and included unsuccessful strategies that tested existing laws. Anthony herself drafted a proposed Sixteenth Amendment granting women the right to vote. The AWSA took a different approach, focusing instead on state-by-state initiatives. Localized approaches proved to be initially more fruitful. Suffrage gains were fought and won one state at a time.

To illustrate these gains, designers crafted infographics in the form of US maps showing which states had adopted suffrage and which ones had not. These infographics tracked suffrage progress, which began in the west and worked its way eastward. "Since larger western states granted the ballot first, the vast map area where suffrage had been won offered a powerful image that suggested the inevitability of their victory," writes historian Allison Lange. Wyoming was first to adopt, in 1869. Then came Utah, Washington, Montana, Colorado, and Idaho. It was a domino effect, and these maps encouraged and legitimized the cascade as it was happening. They were widely reproduced: "The suffrage map became so pervasive in the American landscape that writers and speakers could refer to it without its being present," writes geographer Christina E. Dando.

One of the more beautifully styled examples of these maps comes from Blanche Ames Ames for a suffrage referendum in 1915. In her graphic *The Map Blossoms*, anti-suffrage states are namelessly saturated with ink, while states that had granted women the right to vote are labeled and illustrated with sunflow-ers that can barely be contained. Ames was a famed botanical illustrator, and sunflowers would have been an easily recognizable sign of pro-suffragism; sunflowers were the official state symbol of Kansas, and notable suffragists who campaigned there adopted the flower as an indexical sign of the movement. Massachusetts, New York, New Jersey, and Pennsylvania, on the hopeful cusp of pending ballot measures, are rendered in an absence of either ink or sunflower. Uncle Sam is holding a set of pruning shears to "Prune away Prejudice and these four States will blossom in November." The map is shown growing from a tree whose soil is Liberty, whose pot is Equality, and who is fed and maintained by Justice, Logic, Education, and Truth.

Blanche Ames Ames was an artist, architect, inventor, and women's rights activist. She was highly skilled in aesthetics. When she graduated from Smith College, she set her sights on professional illustration, which she did with a high degree of success. Ames ardently supported women's suffrage and was the art director for the *Woman's Journal and Suffrage News*, where her cartoons, including the map, were published. As her second cousin John S. Ames recalls, "It was inconceivable to her that women weren't granted the same privileges as men. It's 'Goddamnit, women deserve the right to vote!'"

Another suffragist, Bertha Damaris Knobe, drew a more conventional suffrage map for a 1908 *Harper's Weekly* feature spread entitled "Votes for Women: An Object-Lesson." The international map identifies countries across the globe at their respective stages of granting suffrage.

Knobe was born in Indiana. She received her bachelor's degree from Franklin College and went on to become a professional journalist and activist. She wrote for the *Chicago Tribune* but was also deeply committed to the suffrage movement and wrote frequently on such topics. Knobe had an affinity for maps and understood their power. A suffrage map of the United States that she drew in 1907—influenced heavily by a municipal map created by suffragist Anna Nicholes—was so significant it's been called "the suffrage map" of the movement.

Amplifying Women Designers

The first major women's movement in the United States was dedicated to gaining the right to vote. The visual culture of the time of suffrage was instrumental in swaying public opinion and securing those rights. Yet so little of what we have archived, so little of what we use as reference material to shed light on the experience, was made by or attributed to women, let alone women of color or with other intersecting identities. It is incredibly important to hear from women designers themselves and how they chose to represent *their* movement. The work of Evelyn Rumsey Cary, Bertha M. Boyé, Josephine St. Pierre Ruffin, Florida Ruffin Ridley, Katherine Milhous, Mary Shepard Greene Blumenschein, Blanche Ames Ames, and Bertha Damaris Knobe (among others) offers insight into the movement that otherwise cannot be gleaned. My intention is to bring light to these influential women who deserve a place in our canon, yet there is still much work to be done. It is vital to continue to amplify the voices of many different women, all over the globe and throughout history.

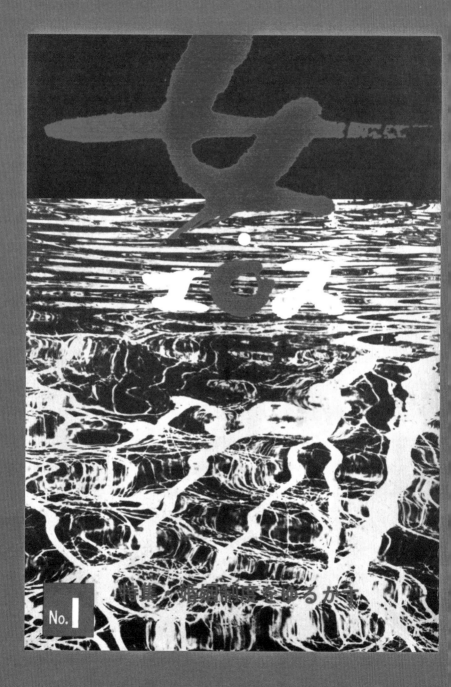

女

エロス

特集　婚姻制度をゆるがす

No. 1

In the Beginning, Woman Was the Sun

Ian Lynam

The time has come to recapture the sun hidden within us. "Reveal the sun hidden within us, reveal the genius hidden within us!" This is the cry we unceasingly cry out to ourselves, the thirst that refuses to be suppressed or quenched, the one instinct that unifies all and sundry instincts and ultimately makes us a complete person. Our savior is the genius within us. We no longer seek our savior in temples or churches, in the Buddha or God. We no longer wait for divine revelation. By our own efforts, we shall lay bare the secrets of nature within us. We shall be our own divine revelation…
— Hiratsuka Raichō, *Seitō* no. 1, 1911

Groundwork

As Japan transitioned from a self-isolated feudal nation with the opening of the country in the late 1800s and into the twentieth century, so did the societal notions of its populace, notably in regard to gender. New roles for women began to appear in the late 1920s, heralding the arrival of the Shōwa era (1926–1989). Previous conceptions of women had aligned with one or more of three archetypes:

Yamauchi Shizuka, cover of *Onna Eros* no. 1, 1973.

the loyal daughter-in-law, the obedient wife, or the devoted mother. During the Shōwa era, state-ordered compulsory basic education paved the way for the emergence of the *jogakusei*, or female student, as the mass mobilization of rural populations to cities uprooted many women from traditional roles.[1] At the same time the boom in clerical and secretarial work cast many as *shokyugō fujin*, or working women.[2] Meanwhile, this differentiation led to the widespread recognition of the role of the housewife, or *shūfu.*

Mass publishing had turned into a giant industry by 1920. The Education System Ordinance, crafted in 1871, had created a marked national increase in literacy for men and women alike, as it made elementary education compulsory, though it wasn't until 1910 that the ordinance became fully implemented. By 1930, more than 90 percent of the Japanese populace had received compulsory education.[3] This, combined with rapid technological developments in printing technology, led to a pronounced desire in the Japanese populace for literature as entertainment.

This resulted in a massive boom in newspapers and magazines from 1918 to 1932, with an increased use of photography. In 1923, the major newspaper *Asahi Shimbun* launched its weekly news magazine, *Asahi Graph*, a large-scale publication that integrated typography, photography, and illustration. Magazines that directly targeted women, including *Fujin Gahō* and *Fujin Graph*, appeared shortly thereafter.[4] These publications were laden with advertising that appealed directly to women, including ads from cosmetics companies such as Shiseido, Kanebo Cosmetics, and Club Cosmetics.[5] Publications for women helped them gain a more developed sense of their roles in society and contributed to defining the intellect and aesthetic of the "new woman."

The most romanticized and also threatening female archetype to emerge in the late Taishō (1912–1926) and early Shōwa eras was the *moga*, the neologism a shorthand for the English *modern girl*. The moga wore bobbed hair akin to Hollywood "It Girl" Clara Bow, often permed or curled (as curling machines became readily available in Japan in the 1920s). She was a city dweller who occupied public spaces; was sexually promiscuous, as exemplified by her deliberate use of makeup and cosmetics; and wore Western-inspired "pajama clothing."[6]

Both the allure and the perceived threat of the moga lay in their ability to think and act freely—to merely *exist* as cosmopolitan beings in opposition to the filial and feudal roles of the daughter-in-law/wife/mother. Perhaps the ultimate archetype of this modern

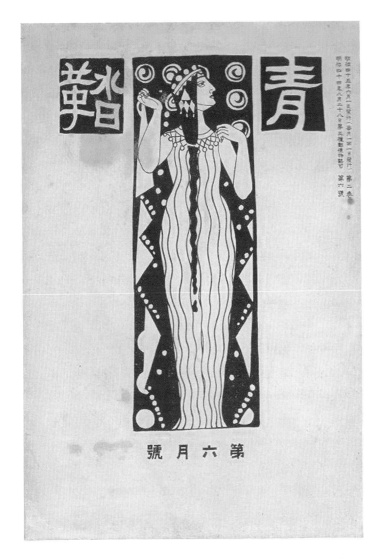

Naganuma Chieko, cover of *Seitō* (Bluestocking), ca. 1911.

girl was the character Naomi from Tanizaki Jun'ichirō's serialized novel *A Fool's Love*, published as *Naomi* in the West. The eponymous character stands in opposition to her husband, Jōji, the book's protagonist. Naomi is sexually aggressive, manipulative, and an insatiable consumer. Over the course of the novel's installments in the *Osaka Morning Press*, starting in 1924,

Naomi shifts from being a subservient, Eurasian-complected fifteen-year-old café waitress to becoming the dominant force in her household, with her husband sleeping in a separate room, simultaneously tormented and in her sexual thrall.

Needless to say, the story of Naomi shocked older readers yet titillated younger audiences while also creating a role model of agency for younger Japanese women. It is notable that Naomi is a café waitress, or *jokyū*, in the beginning of the book, as cafés—some of Japan's first liminal public/private spaces—served as sites for the expression of sexuality, politics, and culture and for the freedom of verbal expression. The café was rivaled by the dancehall, the cinema, and the department store as specific locales where modern Japanese citizens reveled in consumption as much as in forging new modes of thinking about gender, labor, and individuality.[7]

The problem was that most metropolitan women were *not* Naomi, nor did they fall into simple, definable categories of being "traditional" or "modern." Instead they represented and embodied a complex and heady mix of traditional values as much as cosmopolitan desires. A 1925 survey of Ginza, Tokyo's most popular shopping district, by Kon Wajirō and Yoshida Kenkichi—design ethnographers and cofounders of modernology, the study of Tokyo becoming a modern city—showed that two years after the Great Kantō Earthquake, a mere 1 percent of women wore Western-style clothing, as opposed to 67 percent of males who wore Western garb.[8] Neither traditionalism nor modernity were positions that were set in stone in the 1920s, as the design of nationalist propaganda was considered equally as modern as Yanagi Sōetsu's founding of the *mingei* movement, inspired by traditional vernacular pottery.[9]

This plurality was mirrored in the formation of early feminist groups such as the Seitōsha, or Blue Stocking Society, in 1911. The group, consisting of highly educated and largely middle-class women, was led by activist Hiratsuka Raichō. Its name is derived from England's Bluestocking Society, credited with kickstarting first-wave feminism in the West, though the term *bluestocking* would go on to become associated with global feminist movements.[10]

The Seitōsha published the literary magazine *Seitō* (Bluestocking), which, over the course of fifty-two issues, brought women's rights to the fore. *Seitō* was largely designed by visual artist Naganuma Chieko. Its first issue bore an illustration of a heroic woman gazing at the sky, flanked by the two kanji making up the name of the publication. An elongated vertical strip behind the figure and two top quadrants backgrounding the kanji create an abstract kimono.[11]

Issues of *Seitō* became part of the national discourse and debate. However, despite the efforts of the Seitōsha and other early feminist groups in Japan, it was not until 1946, with the creation of a new constitution under the occupation government, that women would receive the right to vote in national elections.

The Rise of Ribu

The mid-1960s saw Japan engaging on a global scale in its export of industrial and manufactured goods. Japan modernized later than many Western nation-states and was therefore able to avoid many of the developmental mishaps that occur during rapid industrialization. This, combined with consistent wage increases for the Japanese labor force, strategic patent acquisitions, improvement of multiple classes of products of foreign origin, and high levels of both private and public investment and savings paved the way to a vastly enhanced economy in the 1970s and '80s.

The middle of 1970 saw the emergence of *Ūman Ribu* (the name represents "Women's Lib(eration)" in the *katakana* writing system). Traditional roles of marriage and family were harshly criticized by Ūman Ribu activists such as Tanaka Mitsu and the Gurūpu Tatakau Onnatachi (Group of Fighting Women), who maintained that the social and cultural structure of Japan oppressed not only women but also men as well.[12] Various Ūman Ribu–oriented groups issued multiple comprehensive critiques of Japanese society that spanned economics, socioeconomic class structures, and historically based, patriarchal cultural constructs.

In 1972, Ūman Ribu organizers cofounded the Ribu Shinjuku Center, a women-run center for feminist activism and women's shelter in Tokyo, where women could receive legal assistance and counseling on reproductive health. In many ways, members of the more than fifty Ribu cells that spread throughout Japan were far more radical than Western feminists, with some holding pro-infanticide positions and espousing extremes of sexual liberation. Yet the movement occasionally tended toward more conservative ideologies; when individuals associated with the Ribu movement translated the American books *Women's Liberation: Blueprint for the Future* (1971) and *Our Bodies, Ourselves* (1974) into Japanese, they intentionally omitted the chapters devoted to lesbian identity. It wasn't until the 1980s that the text on lesbian identity from the 1984 edition of *Our Bodies, Ourselves* was included as a two-page insert in the Japanese publication.[13]

The cover of the first edition of the English-language *Our Bodies, Ourselves* features a photograph

A spread from *Onna Eros* showing an Ūman Ribu member at a march, 1973.

of three women of differing generations holding a placard reading "Women Unite," surrounded by awkward hand lettering. The cover of the first Japanese edition is both more abstract and more aesthetically refined. The kanji for *woman* is the largest character in the title; it is offset by an orange spot-color illustration of a sun against a striped silver background.

Collectively, the members of the Ribu Shinjuku Center produced the radical feminist magazine *Onna Eros* beginning in 1973; it was published by the Tokyo-based left-wing Shakai Hyoronsha publishing group. In *Onna Eros*, numerous contributors sought to eliminate the prewar stratification of women by age, class, and occupation and instead align them all under the term *onna* ("women"). Edited by Yōko Miki and Yōko Saeki, the first issue of the magazine included wide-ranging topics under the general theme of "Unsettling the Marital System." The issue included historical examinations of expressions of feminism globally, a reprint of Hiratsuka Raichō's manifesto from the first issue of the *Seitō* journal in 1911, a feature on progressive feminist groups in the United States, op-ed essays

1971年 8月　第一回リブ合宿（長野県）

A photographic spread from the 1973 inaugural issue of *Onna Eros* depicting Ribu activists in solidarity during the very first Ribu camping convention.

on the preference of many women to remain single and on the liberation of sex, and an essay on lesbian identity.

The cover design for the first issue of *Onna Eros* was executed by Yamauchi Shizuka, who was also responsible for the masthead logo, which would be used throughout the entire print run of the magazine. The journal's editorial design was handled by Asuka Kyoka. Professionally typeset, *Onna Eros* legitimized the Ribu movement in print. The phototype layouts integrated photographs and illustrations from contributors, spot illustrations, and photographic sections depicting members of the movement speaking at Ribu conferences, pursuing direct action through "die-in" public protests, and being physically assaulted by males. Of note is a photograph printed across a double-page spread in the magazine's inaugural issue. It shows ten naked Ribu-associated women, the majority arm in arm, standing in a copse of trees amid tall, wild grasses during the first Ribu camping convention (women only, members of the press included) in 1971—women together, in nature. Accompanying the photograph were illustrations by Usu Nanami and inline illustrations by Kusano Mutsuko and Kunii Isako.

Onna Eros was only one of scores of Ribu-oriented publications that emerged under the name *onna no mini-comi* or "women's mini communication" ("mini communication" being the opposite of "mass communication") from all over Japan. These included titles such as the Tokyo letterpress-printed booklet *This Road*; the Osaka-based *From Women to Women*; translations of essays culled from the first two issues of the periodical *Notes*, edited by the Canadian American writer Shulamith Firestone; and the Tokyo journal *Neo-Ribu* (Journal of women's liberation). The often gritty analogue aesthetics of handwrought illustration, printmaking, hand lettering, and press type; the small-press approach; and the organic distribution networks of the original onna no mini-comi—in essence, proto-zines, as much as short books—left a DIY imprint that would be mirrored unconsciously in the perzine (personal zine), Riot Grrrl, queercore, and general fanzine movements that sprang out of the feminist and queer forks of the hardcore punk scene globally in the 1990s.

Cover of *From Women to Women*, 1973, translations of essays culled from the first two issues of the periodical *Notes*, edited by the Canadian American writer Shulamith Firestone.

The most vocal leader of the Ribu movement, Tanaka Mitsu, ceased publishing and participating in public activism in 1975, when she moved to Mexico after visiting a United Nations conference there. She lived there for four years and became a single mother during that time. In her absence, the Ribu Shinjuku Center closed in 1977, though Ribu-oriented publications continued in earnest. *Onna Eros* ceased publication in 1983; other publications continued

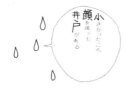

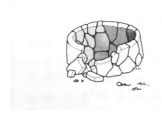

The cover of the fourth issue of Kuno Ayako's zine
***Woman's Mutiny*, 1972, published in Nagoya, Japan.**

publication through the early 2010s. Kuno Ayako (a Ribu member from Nagoya who had been present at the first camping convention) published fifty-nine issues of the A5-sized seventy-page zine *Woman's Mutiny* between 1971 and 2013. It began with a print run of two thousand copies, though the last issue saw the number reduced to five hundred.

Independent feminist-oriented small-press initiatives—such as *Lilmag*, a zine run in Tokyo by Nonaka Momo—continue today. The website for Nonaka's DIY venture lists the publications they carry as being both zines and mini-comi—a contemporary paean to the heyday of Ribu.[14]

Note: All names in this essay are included according to Japanese standards, with family name first and given name second.

1982 first year of national Transformation

Collective Authorship and Shared Process: The Madame Binh Graphics Collective

Aggie Toppins

In graphic design history, the word *revolution* has typically described periods of formal experimentation, like constructivism and de Stijl, or technological change, as in the "digital revolution."[1] In the margins of this history are "political graphics," such as state propaganda and witty protest posters that sit comfortably, if peripherally, near the central commercial canon. It is in the margins of these margins where the real revolutions are. In the less explored spaces where design meets dissent, where art practice converges with direct action—this is where we find the Madame Binh Graphics Collective.

From 1977 until 1983, the Brooklyn-based Madame Binh Graphics Collective (MBGC) produced agitprop in solidarity with Black liberation and what were then called "Third World" liberation movements. MBGC was an affiliate of the May 19th Communist Organization, an all-White, ultra-left, anti-racist, and anti-imperialist group. Members Mary Patten, Laura Whitehorn, Margo Pelletier, Wendy Grossman, Lisa Roth, Eve Rosahn, and Donna Borup named their alliance after the South Vietnamese

Robert Mugabe with the Madame Binh Graphics Collective: ZANU Women's League print, 1982, poster.

Communist leader Madame Nguyen Thi Bình.

Their story, as Patten describes in her memoir, *Revolution as an Eternal Dream*, is one of "exemplary failure."[2] MBGC wanted nothing less than a new world order. It engaged in a radical politics that demanded the release of political prisoners, the end of White supremacy, and the renunciation of capitalist power. Of course, it did not achieve this. Its members paid a steep price for trying—eventually becoming political prisoners themselves—and were nearly erased from history as a consequence. MBGC is worth remembering as a case study in feminist methodology and the complexities of allyship.

MBGC practiced in a tumultuous political context from which the wellspring of activist art was tapped. Political historian Dan Berger describes the decade of the group's awakening as a time of "exploding limits."[3] In the 1970s, the Vietnam War intensified and ended after myriad student protests, including the shootings at Kent State. On the heels of the civil rights movement, Black power came to prominence with the revolutionary sects the Black Panther Party and the Black Liberation Army. The US Supreme Court ruling in *Roe v. Wade* made abortion legal, a win for women's liberation. At the same time, this movement was newly challenged by thinkers like Audre Lorde, bell hooks, and the Combahee River Collective, who expanded feminism through intersections with queerness and

Republic of New Afrika

Madame Binh Graphics Collective and the Republic of New Afrika, *Assata Shakur Is Welcome Here!*, 1979, poster.

racial oppression. Following the Stonewall Riots, LGBTQ liberation and pride became more public, even as the first openly gay elected official in California, Harvey Milk, was assassinated. The US federal government launched the "war on drugs" and increased mass incarceration, which devastated Black communities. Capital punishment was abolished and reinstated. There were prison revolts and violent police retaliations.

Economic neoliberalism and Cold War politics gripped mainstream society and dominated media bias. Artists began to turn away from the "white cube" and toward the streets as the site for political discourse. While some collectives addressed the art world through politics, the Madame Binh Graphics Collective used art as an instrument for politics. This was an era before the fall of the USSR; socialism was still perceived to be a real possibility. For hundreds of activist groups, it was literally worth fighting for.

MBGC members were not professional designers. They were politically minded artists or artistically inclined activists. They worked in two primary modes of production, both aimed at jolting White people into anti-racist action. In one mode, they produced limited-edition, multicolor serigraphs, such as *Attica: The Struggle Continues*. These were sold at art exhibitions to raise "material aid" for liberation movements. In their other mode, MBGC made fliers, T-shirts, and stickers, which members distributed publicly to create awareness about liberation struggles. These were expediently produced using silk screen, mimeograph, or the group's own small offset press.

While many of its projects were self-initiated, MBGC also ghost-designed for comrades in the revolution. MBGC used its resources and skills to give form to a collaborator's message. Following activist Assata Shakur's escape from prison, the Black separatist organization the Republic of New Afrika asked MBGC to create a sign of sanctuary: *Assata Shakur Is Welcome Here!* These flyers were distributed through a network of supporters and posted in windows throughout New York City. The byline credits the Republic of New Afrika, not Madame Binh Graphics Collective; MBGC did not usually sign its work or take credit for lending support to peer organizations.

MBGC's methodology was itself a stand against patriarchy. At the start of a project, the members would meet to discuss goals and priorities. Then, each member would independently sketch ideas. They would regroup for critique, assess options, and choose a direction together. They would appoint a "lead designer," usually the woman whose idea had been selected, and the other members would support her, with members taking turns leading and following one another. This process may seem familiar to designers who have worked in small agencies, but in the contexts of the male-dominated art world and revolutionary groups alike, such a nonhierarchical process was atypical.

Pairing concrete skills with revolutionary ideas was central to MBGC's vision for lasting change, as it was for other feminist political organizations such as the London-based See Red Women's Workshop or the Chicago Women's Liberation Union.[4] MBGC taught silkscreen techniques to women at its studio. Students made individual projects and contributed to collaborative ones, adopting MBGC's way of discussion and evaluation. MBGC members gave presentations about the content of revolutionary art and the necessity of collective work. They connected women's liberation to liberation efforts worldwide. "The ability to make a powerful and vivid political statement through the use of silk-screen is an important part of building a movement that can win," reads a recruitment flyer. "As women struggling against our enemy, U.S. imperialism, we want to participate in a culture that resists and fights for human rights."[5]

MBGC aesthetics followed from its socialist values and its desire to cede power in a White supremacist society to Black people and other people of color. Cultural quotation was common among political revolutionaries who disavowed private property. The Black Panther Party (BPP), for example, was in visual dialogue with OSPAAAL, the Cuban Organization of Solidarity with the People of Asia, Africa & Latin America. In 1968, following the assassination of Dr. Martin Luther King Jr., OSPAAAL designer Alfredo Rostgaard created a poster on which the words *Black Power* were set between the pointed teeth of a red-eyed panther. BPP later used this same graphic, replacing the words *Black Power* with an image of Huey Newton, the party's cofounder, who had been imprisoned. OSPAAAL returned the homage by featuring illustrations by Emory Douglas, BPP's minister of culture, in their publications and posters. Such borrowing was not considered plagiarism, but a way of signifying alliances.[6]

Grassroots movements such as MBGC also made historical and cultural references. The Berkeley Political Poster Workshop, an anti–Vietnam War student group working in the early 1970s, referred to the prints of Spanish artist Francisco Goya as well as to those of the Atelier Populaire of the Paris 1968 riots. The Chicago

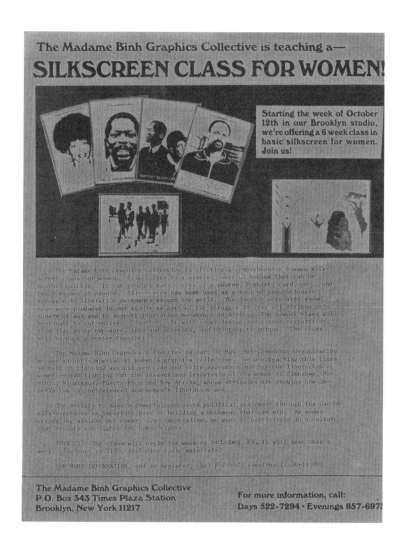

Madame Binh Graphics Collective,
Silkscreen Class for Women, **1979, flyer.**

Women's Graphics Collective wholly
re-created *Lipstick*, a poster designed
by Cuban artist José Gómez Fresquet
that juxtaposed an image of a White woman applying lipstick with
one of a bloody-nosed Vietnamese woman. The symbolism embed-
ded in these graphics formed a lexicon for political expression.

MBGC similarly used extant cultural material as an activist
vocabulary. It drew subject matter from Chinese peasant paintings
and lifted psychedelic color schemes from Cuban propaganda. The

influence of German artist John Heartfield is evident in MBGC's use of drawing as montage, as seen in *Support Black Liberation*.[7] MBGC often grouped small portraits of leading figures into a cascading composition. In these montages, individuals are clearly discernible, but they are visually and metaphorically inseparable from the mass.

Activist intertextuality was coeval with the rise of postmodernism. While postmodern artists and designers were also inclined to quotation, their poaching was meant to undermine originality or to issue ironic critiques. MBGC was not engaged in this discourse.[8] It used well-known motifs to amplify an earnest message of struggle and liberation, participating in an ecosystem of signs that communicated the revolution with urgency.

Although MBGC had no signature style, its approach, as Patten describes it, was "realist," meaning that the group used representational imagery combined with succinct, actionable language.[9] Compared to the abstractions of the art world, MBGC's work was unambiguous. Its posters directly addressed an audience imagined as White people, whom it hoped to organize into a mass movement.[10]

As White people, MBGC members identified themselves as inheritors of empire. They wished to commit a racialized version of class suicide.[11] While mainstream feminists chanted "the personal is political," MBGC members dissolved their individuality into the collective struggle. As a result, they exhausted themselves. Impatient for change, they worked day and night for the revolution, ate poorly, and slept beneath the toxic fumes of their drying prints. In hindsight, Laura Whitehorn notes, this dismissal of self-care was a misinterpretation of priorities.[12]

MBGC's incredible enthusiasm came with a dose of humility. Patten recalls that the group was sometimes criticized for its renderings of Black people, a lesson in "always-dreaded always-already-there racism" that deepened the members' sense of responsibility.[13] Over time, MBGC doubled down on design by committee. What little independence existed within MBGC's methodology gradually disappeared. Every decision about form and content came to be legislated by the entire organization.[14] It became isolated in its zeal and unrelatable to the audiences it hoped to reach. Eventually, MBGC abandoned participation in exhibitions for an all-consuming political existence.[15]

At JFK Airport in 1981, several key members of MBGC were involved in a protest of the South African national rugby team, the Springboks, whose world tour was globally interpreted as support

Madame Binh Graphics Collective, *Support Black Liberation*, **1978, poster.**

for apartheid. Their plan was to drop homemade stink bombs on the floor of the Springboks' plane. But an altercation with police resulted in a jar of acid landing on an officer's face, partially blinding him. Five MBGC members were arrested.[16]

When one of the members was found to be linked to the 1981 robbery of a Brink's armored car that resulted in three deaths, group participants were reindicted under riot charges and their bail raised to $100,000. The district attorney evoked the Racketeer Influenced and Corrupt Organizations Act (RICO) so that no one could post bail for them without submitting to an investigational hearing. From 1981 until 1983, most of the Madame Binh Graphics Collective was jailed on Rikers Island. Meanwhile, police in search of information about the May 19th Communist Organization raided the MBGC studio, poured sand in its press, and destroyed its work.

In jail, MBGC members continued to build community and make art, often with little more to work with than toothpaste and magazine clippings. They drew portraits of fellow inmates, who sometimes sent the images home as a way of staying in touch with their families. They produced "defense committee" propaganda, including fiery rhetoric that advocated for their own release.[17]

Patten noted that while behind bars, MBGC members returned to their individual identities.[18] By 1983, most members had moved on to new pursuits. In some cases, their privilege as White women manifested in their ability to chart new careers after prison. Yet each woman remained an activist. Lisa Roth relocated to San Francisco. Mary Patten moved to Chicago, went to graduate school, and became an art professor. Wendy Grossman became an art historian. Margo Pelletier worked as a printer at Robert Blackburn Printmaking Workshop before moving on to the Dia Art Foundation. Eve Rosahn became a public defender. Laura Whitehorn served a fourteen-year sentence for charges related to the 1983 bombing of the US Capitol by a group affiliated with the May 19th Communist Organization. Today, she is an editor at *POZ* magazine. Donna Borup failed to appear in court in 1982, following the Springboks incident. She remains a fugitive to this day.

Despite its deep commitment to political change, the Madame Binh Graphics Collective is not usually remembered in histories of art and activism, let alone histories of graphic design. In their time, the members were so absorbed by their work that they did not take time to promote themselves for posterity. In recent years, however, MBGC's work has surfaced in exhibitions at national venues.[19]

Patten partially attributes MBGC's invisibility to its sectarianism.[20] Critic Gregory Sholette observed, "When artists engage in direct political action, the artworld tends to respond with renunciation or denial."[21] MBGC's extremism may have made its story initially unpalatable.[22]

Yet in the context of the 1970s, state-sanctioned violence was broadcast at unprecedented levels. In a world in which the Vietnam War was possible, in which police routinely brutalized Black protesters, and in which students could be murdered for demonstrating on their own campus, violence was quotidian. Given that this upheaval rhymes so closely with our current time, we may question what has been historically dismissed as too extreme. MBGC's omission from history is a prompt for us to examine who, as Whitehorn asks, gets to define violence.[23]

By emphasizing materiality and form, design historians often bestow objects with a misleading autonomy that upstages their use in society.[24] Under glass, MBGC's outcomes do not reveal the significance of their methodology, nor do they speak of their complex negotiations between politics and aesthetics. MBGC's story also beckons us to ask: How should White people become allies in the struggle for racial equality? In MBGC's time, the term *ally* wasn't used. The members saw themselves not as supportive friends but as coconspirators in the revolution. They put their bodies on the line. They staged spectacles that they hoped would "take the pressure off" oppressed communities and place more responsibility on White people.[25]

In Patten's observation, activists today "tend to refuse the spectacle of shock and awe" in favor of "an aesthetics of duration, stillness, and slowing-down."[26] Following the 1970s surge of activist art, the field of socially engaged art developed. Rather than wielding the blunt instrument of propaganda, today's socially engaged artists often deploy care-based forms of collective action that treat the social itself as the medium for change.[27]

Two contemporary examples are the Baltimore-based publishing initiative Press Press and the Women's Center for Creative Work (WCCW), located in Los Angeles. Like MBGC before them, these organizations engage in anti-racist and anti-imperialist work through nonpatriarchal models. They provide platforms for oppressed voices through printed matter and programming based on discussion and skill sharing. Unlike MBGC, both are intersectional organizations that model the world they wish to see rather than stage attacks on the world as it is.[28]

In its "Toolkit for Cooperative, Collective, and Collaborative Cultural Work," Press Press distinguishes *explicit hierarchies*, which are agreed upon ahead of time by members of the group, from *embodied hierarchies*, which are forms of entitlement bestowed by class, race, gender, etc.[29] The group writes, "It is crucial to build a culture of open and courageous communication between group members in order to be able to thoughtfully negotiate the tensions and anxieties that may arise around explicit and embodied hierarchies."[30] In this view, hierarchies can be useful when leadership is defined as a rotating role disassociated with power over others. The Madame Binh Graphics Collective initially lived by this pact.

Press Press also asserts that personal growth and continuous dialogue are essential to the health of the collective. Similarly, it is among the core values of the Women's Center for Creative Work to cultivate a spirit of "hospitality and care."[31] WCCW encourages "self-determined" participation, asking members to take care of themselves in order to best handle conflict while engaging in the work of restorative justice. Holding space for self-care in political activism was a lesson that MBGC learned the hard way.

What endures from the Madame Binh Graphics Collective is the knowledge that politics and aesthetics often exist in an ambivalent relationship. Through the traces left by history's eraser, in the margins of the margins, MBGC complicates creative practice within a broader ethical domain that encircles allyship and privilege. Its example allows us to reflect on what it really means to be revolutionary with graphic design.

FIGHT RACISM!
FIGHT IMPERIALISM!

**ANTI-IMPERIALIST PAPER OF THE
REVOLUTIONARY COMMUNIST GROUP**

ISSUE No 3 MARCH/APRIL 1980
PRICE 20p

ISSN 0143 7828

VICTORY!

Photograph – Associated Press, supplied by International Defence and Aid Fund

We salute the landslide victory of ZANU and ZAPU in the Zimbabwean elections. It will give an enormous impetus to the struggle against the racist apartheid regime in South Africa. This overwhelming victory will be joyfully greeted by the Irish people fighting against the same ruthless British imperialism. A body blow to the British ruling class it is a great step forward for the British working class and the world-wide movement against imperialism.

Despite the enormous obstacles placed in its way by the British state and the racist Rhodesian regime the Patriotic Front has won 77 out of 80 seats. The imperialist puppet Muzorewa won 3 seats thus demonstrating conclusively that the Muzorewa regime existed solely by virtue of the backing it received from Britain and South Africa.

British Imperialism Exposed

How thoroughly the Patriotic Front's overwhelming victory exposes British imperialism! The British had claimed that the Patriotic Front had no mass support, that it existed by intimidating the Zimbabwean masses, that the Patriotic Front forces were 'terrorists' and 'criminals'. The British state has made the exact same claim about every liberation movement it has confronted. It says the same about the Provisional Republican Movement in Ireland today. It attempts to justify its own terror, torture and repression of Irish republicans on these very same grounds.

Britain Stacked the Odds

It was the military strength and mass support

And now the Patriotic Front victory reveals the truth – that the Zimbabwean masses have all along supported the Patriotic Front; that despite the enormous repression they have suffered at the hands of the Rhodesian racist regime the people's support for the Patriotic Front was unshakeable and steadfast; that the war against the Patriotic Front waged by imperialism and its racist allies in Rhodesia and South Africa was *in reality* designed to crush the masses and prevent them from exercising their right to self determination.

What a humiliating blow has been struck at British imperialism! The victory in Zimbabwe shouts its message round the world – that British state lied about the Patriotic Front just as it has lied about every liberation movement and just as today it lies about the Provisional Republican Movement. British imperialism stands revealed as a bloody handed liar!

for the Patriotic Front which forced Britain to the negotiating table and forced Britain to hold elections. The British plan was to use the Lancaster House settlement to stack all the odds against the Patriotic Front and thus try to secure their defeat. During the run up to the election, as the Zimbabwean masses openly and defiantly proclaimed that the Patriotic Front was *their* movement, the British state resorted more and more to the same techniques of naked repression that it uses against the Irish people today.

While the Patriotic Front military forces were in assembly camps the Rhodesian army and the hated auxiliaries were allowed to roam the country freely. At no time did Britain make any attempt to restrict the Rhodesian army to base, yet every ounce of British propaganda concerned the 'difficulty' of getting all the Patriotic Front forces to assembly camps and of the so-called 'intimidation' by the Patriotic Front. The reality was that the Rhodesian army, the notorious Selous scouts, the police and the auxiliaries were able, *with British help* to conduct an intensified campaign of repression and intimidation against the masses.

● Robert Mugabe was the subject of repeated assassination attempts. His home was the target of a grenade attack (as were many ZANU officials' homes) and an expert attempt to blow up his car was made.

● Two Selous scouts blew themselves up whilst about to bomb a fourth church in Harare, their intention being to plant the blame for this on ZANU.

● On several occasions the Rhodesian army shot and killed groups of freedom fighters on their way to assembly camps. For example, a ZANLA commander leading 118 men to link up with the ceasefire monitoring force was arrested along with all his men. The authorities have only accounted for the whereabouts of 22 of them. These are in prison.

● By the time of the election the police under Soames' directions had detained no less than 10,000 ZANU and ZAPU supporters including leading officials and candidates.

● At Umvuma a busload of people were returning from a ZANU rally. They were all arrested and beaten up and forced to sign an admission of guilt. Events of that kind were *continued on page 3*

FINE WORDS FOUL DEEDS
FALSE FRIENDS

Black and immigrant workers in Britain suffer from a dual oppression both from racism and class exploitation. In resisting this oppression they are forced into direct confrontation with the British state. This has placed black and immigrant workers in the vanguard of the struggle for the overthrow of the British imperialist state.

With the growing crisis of imperialism the 'open enemies' of the working class, the unashamed racists and pro-imperialists are increasingly being exposed, The challenge to imperialism will grow deeper as unemployment, poverty and repression become the only prospects for larger and larger sections of the working class. The continued existence of the imperialist system more and more rests on the influence of the *false friends* – opportunist currents within the labour movement which attempt to reconcile the working class to the capitalist system. These opportunist currents drawn from the relatively privileged layers of the working class argue that imperialism need not be violent; that the British state can act in a democratic fashion for the benefit of all classes; that the present crisis can be solved by 'alternative' economic plans in the interest of the working class. These opportunist layers are terrified by the revolutionary intransigence of the oppressed because such intransigence threatens to challenge the imperialist system and so undermine the basis of their secure and privileged existence.

In the last issue of this paper (Jan/Feb 1980) we showed how the newly emerging black vanguard in Britain had begun to undermine these opportunist currents in the working class movement. Sunday 25 November 1979, at a demonstration of over 20,000 people against

racism, saw Manjit Singh, chairman of the Asian Youth Movement Bradford and Suresh Grover speaking on behalf of the Southall Defence Committee attack Tony Benn for the racist policies of the Labour government. This won support from thousands of black people.

The petit bourgeois socialist left in Britain, faced with such a determined stand against the Labour Party, simply censored it away. Not one of the CP, SWP, IMG mentioned this important event in their newspaper reports. (see FRFI 2 Jan/Feb 1980)

Another political stand taken by this emerging black vanguard has been its consistent support for the Irish people's war against British imperialism. On the anniversary of Bloody Sunday this year we witnessed an uncompromising call by a speaker from AYMB for the 'victory of the IRA'. Again this was followed by an embarrassed silence from the petit bourgeois socialist left – the CP, SWP and the IMG, who are renowned for their attacks on the Provisional Republican Movement (and indeed all anti-imperialist movements).

The revolutionary voice of black people continues to be raised and is gathering strength. With the AYMB's organisation of a Black Freedom March in June and the call for the building of a national black organisation, the petit bourgeois left can no longer simply censor such important developments. It has been forced to respond.

The publication of the IMG's latest conference document *The Struggle for Black Liber-*

ation (Socialist Challenge 21 February 1980) is their response. It reveals the intentions of the petit bourgeois left in relation to the emerging revolutionary vanguard. They are trying as we shall see to *undermine it and drag it back* from the revolutionary road it has taken.

The Struggle for Black Liberation marks a change in the position of the IMG. Its new position is couched in extremely revolutionary language which tries to conceal its thoroughly *continued on page 3*

Typeset by Red Lion Setters (TU) 22 Brownlow Mews, London WC1
Printed by Newsline Press Ltd (TU) Nation House, Balmoral Road, Watford, Herts.
© World Copyright: RCG Publications Ltd March 1980

Typist to Typesetter: Norma Kitson and Her Red Lion Setters

Ruth Sykes

Red Lion Setters (RLS) has the reputation of having been a radical female typesetting collective that operated in London from 1973 to the late 1980s.[1] It was founded by the White South African Norma Kitson (1933–2002), who was driven to the United Kingdom by the South African authorities' intolerance of her links with the African National Congress (ANC) and the South African Communist Party (SACP).[2] RLS did both paid work for socialist, academic, and feminist publishers and donated work to support the political concerns of Kitson and other RLS workers.[3] RLS is mentioned in passing within histories of women in print; it's worth spending more time on its story as a case study of typesetting affording women political agency.[4]

Megan Dobney, a typographer and designer in the 1970s, recalls that women typesetters and all-female typesetting shops were rare at that time.[5] According to Dobney, records of the National Graphical Association (the union that represented typographers and associated trades in the UK) show that just 6 percent of its members were female in the mid-1960s.

Carol Brickley, designer, *Fight Facisim, Fight Imperialism*, March/April 1980.

95

While not all typesetters were unionized, it is safe to treat Dobney's recollection as accurate.

Yet, as typesetting labor became increasingly mechanized, thus requiring less physical strength, there were challenges to typesetting as a "man's job," driven by concerns both commercial and egalitarian. In 1843, promotional material for the Young and Delcambre type composer pictured a woman sitting at the keyboard of the machine, thereby proving the simplicity and cheapness of the process (a woman can do it!).[6] In 1860, printer and publisher Emily Faithfull established London's Victoria Press to employ women as typesetters.[7] Sexist ideologies about women's roles prevailed into the twentieth century, however, both outside and within a trade that involved working with metal.[8]

In the late 1960s and into the 1970s, the computerization of the typesetting process rendered the process two dimensional and

NON-STOP

OUTSIDE SOUTH AFRICA HOUSE TRAFALGAR SQUARE

PICKET

- RELEASE NELSON MANDELA
- RELEASE ALL SOUTH AFRICAN POLITICAL PRISONERS
- CLOSE DOWN THE RACIST SOUTH AFRICAN EMBASSY

19 APRIL

DEMONSTRATE

Assemble 2pm
Bidborough St, Nearest tube
Kings Cross.

MARCH TO TRAFALGAR SQUARE TO START THE NON-STOP PICKET AT 4PM

CITY OF LONDON ANTI-APARTHEID GROUP   Tel 837-6050 FOR DETAILS
FUNDED BY THE GLC

City of London Anti-Apartheid Group, leaflet promoting the "non-stop picket" for the release of "all South African political prisoners" begun in 1986. This was likely to have been produced by Carol Brickley at her own business, Boldface, which she set up after working at Red Lion Setters.

the work even less physical. The typesetter's computer keyboard adopted the secretarial-standard QWERTY layout, familiar to many women but alien to many men. Women's long association with QWERTY keyboards had existed since the late nineteenth century, when office work had become feminized.[9]

In 1975, UK legislation made it unlawful to discriminate in employment opportunities on the basis of sex, but discrimination did not disappear.[10] In her autobiography, Kitson describes the difficulty of finding secure employment in any role as she approached her forties, due to age discrimination.[11] But for women with access to money, the latest technological changes to typesetting and the associated dramatic reduction in the cost of equipment meant that a small typesetting business could be set up with an investment of around £2,000 (today's $33,500)—the price of Kitson's first IBM composer, bought in 1973. It would have taken two years for the average British woman working full time to earn that sum, so it was not an option for most.[12] Kitson obtained the money as a loan from a family friend.

Advertisements in the feminist magazine *Spare Rib* suggest that other UK women of the era similarly had access to typesetting equipment. Examples include ads for By Women For Women, which listed typesetting along with a raft of other traditionally male-gendered services like "DIY," electrical work, and gardening; Caroline MacKechnie and Shirley Divers, who offered "IBM Typesetting" with "good rates for feminist/alternative books, mags, pamphlets, etc." along with "illustration and paste up services"; and Dark Moon (cofounded by Helen Lowe) and Bread 'n' Roses, two workers' collectives.[13]

Although Red Lion Setters entered this scene and has been characterized as an all-woman collective, it should be noted that this description is not strictly true. Gail Cartmail, a typesetter and trade union activist, recalls working at RLS alongside a male colleague in the 1980s. She does not remember evidence of a truly collective business structure at RLS, in the sense of workers jointly owning the organization and equally benefiting from the flat-pay system.[14]

Why did Kitson establish Red Lion Setters? In her autobiography, she states that in 1973 she was in need of secure employment. When a commission-only job in a nonunionized typesetting firm was offered, she had no choice but to take it. Her efforts to unionize that workplace led to her firing, but the experience showed Kitson that her skills as a typist were enough to transform her into a typesetter—a job requiring a similar skill set but providing a much improved rate of pay. Rather than continue to battle to find employment, Kitson established Red Lion Setters.

In addition to requiring money, setting up a typesetting service demands knowledge of the graphic reproduction process and its business administration, as well as entrée into a network of paying clients. Kitson's previous political and professional life provided that. In Kitson's obituary, journalist Denis Herbstein writes that Kitson learned printing skills when she joined the South African Communist Party in her twenties.[15] Kitson's autobiography reveals that during her thirties, as bookkeeper and then company director at F. H. K. Henrion's Studio H, Kitson acquired valuable business skills in a print design environment. Her entry to the middle-class publishing network required to build a general typesetting business may also have been facilitated by the privileged social milieu Kitson inhabited, following an affluent childhood, private education, and international travel prior to settling in the UK.

Kitson saw typesetting as a way not only to earn a wage but also to contribute to the work of the anti-apartheid movement. She expressed her hope that RLS could be a free-of-charge typesetting unit for the African National Congress (ANC) in London, with Kitson's paying clients covering her salary and business costs. The ANC declined this offer, however. Kitson recounts that her skills were put to use within the ANC in less prominent ways: she trained the leader of the new ANC technical unit and herself was given low-profile work, such as "typing document briefs, and even books for black leaders and students, who came to me direct."[16] As a member of the ANC Women's Committee Propaganda Subcommittee, she turned her typesetting skills to producing leaflets, cards, and documents.[17]

Did Kitson intend to empower women with her majority-female workplace? Cartmail suggests that Kitson's motivation for majority-female hires stemmed from her desire to take a matriarchal approach to leadership, which perhaps was easier to carry out in a female environment.[18] Second-wave feminism, ascendant in the 1970s, did not appear a prime motivator for Kitson, and the force of the wave may have been more of an enabling, rather than driving, one, allowing Kitson to set up her organization to suit her management style.

Gail Cartmail recalls that she was attracted to Red Lion Setters by the opportunity to donate work to the anti-apartheid cause. Further, RLS helped Cartmail develop an internationalist approach within the trade union movement, as there she met members of the South African Congress of Trade Unions. These comrades inspired Cartmail's later campaign to persuade British colleagues in the National Graphical Association to support an anti-apartheid motion to expel the South African Typographical Union from the International Graphical Federation.[19]

Other benefits Cartmail acknowledges from working at Red Lion Setters include the generally hospitable environment and agreeable content of the commercial work. "On a good day, working at RLS was pleasant," she says. "It had a nice atmosphere, within a tasteful conversion of an industrial space in Clerkenwell. The office was nicely set out, the kitchen was a pleasant place for lunch."[20] Working as a jobbing typesetter in the general trade did not always allow politically conscious typesetters to work on palatable commercial material, but RLS did, with clients including the *London Review of Books*, *History Workshop Journal*, and *Screen* magazine.[21]

In part, Cartmail viewed working at RLS as a relief from the rest of the industry, recalling a previous, nonunionized workplace as somewhat exploitative, with the business owner linking himself up to his typesetting room with a funnel so he could listen in on workers. In contrast, RLS was generally a benevolent workplace and supported trade unionism—in spirit, at least. Cartmail notes RLS did not always adhere to union rules. Weighing the benefits of producing politically important work against the flexible approach to union rules was a balancing act that not all unionized typesetters could perform for very long. Cartmail's employment at RLS was short term.

A longer-serving employee was Carol Brickley (1947–2019), who began working at Red Lion Setters in 1976.[22] Active in radical left-wing politics prior to joining RLS, Brickley helped found the UK's Revolutionary Communist Group (RCG) in 1974 and stayed at its forefront for decades. Brickley was closely involved with RCG's newspaper, *Fight Racism! Fight Imperialism!*, first issued in 1979 (issue no. 3 is pictured on page 94). She is credited by the group for forty years of influential contribution to the publication's editorial direction, graphic design, and production. The paper's design template remains even today largely as Brickley designed it in the 1970s.[23] Cartmail recalls that Red Lion Setters did favors for the production of this publication, and it's possible that working within the print production field enhanced Brickley's already substantial contribution to the radical left. Her writing for the publication is a record of her political thought leadership and her contributions to the history of the RCG.[24] After developing typesetting skills at Red Lion Setters and learning related management skills via promotion to RLS company director, Brickley set up her own typesetting and design business, Boldface.[25]

Kitson may have felt sidelined by the London ANC, but her personal activism benefited from both her typesetting skill and the support of her colleagues at Red Lion Setters. Cartmail remembers Kitson's charisma and the influence it had on colleagues. These practical and people skills were part of a wider arsenal of publicity weapons that Kitson deployed with remarkable outcomes during the 1980s. In 1982, when Kitson discovered that her son, Steven, had been detained in South Africa when visiting his imprisoned father, David Kitson (who was serving a twenty-year sentence related to his involvement with the anti-apartheid and communist movements), Red Lion Setters' staff powered the campaign to free Steven.[26] Telephone calls were made, leaflets were produced, and campaign roles were filled by RLS workers. The campaign was covered on national television news, and within days Steven was released.[27]

Norma Kitson and Carol Brickley then founded the City of London Anti-Apartheid Group (CAAG), which was famed for two nonstop, round-the-clock protests outside of the South African embassy in London, taking place in 1982 and 1986–90.[28] CAAG needed a flow of publicity material and newsletters to keep up the momentum of the pickets and its own momentum. Typesetting skills and equipment, which in the 1980s were not the almost instant-access resources of today, were assets for this political activity. Pictured on page 96 is a leaflet, possibly designed and produced by Brickley, to promote the second nonstop picket that began in 1986.[29]

Did Red Lion Setters extend their support to political publications beyond the anti-apartheid cause? The editors of *m/f: a feminist journal* (1978–1986) typeset by RLS, are evidently full of gratitude for the help they received in the production of their journal. *m/f* editor Parveen Adams recalls, "We worked long hours editing articles and composing issues—all in the days of the typewriter and Sellotape."[30] The journal's website confirms, "We have always felt a deep gratitude to Norma Kitson and Red Lion Setters, our typesetters from the beginning," and *m/f* editor Elizabeth Cowie insists the editors' vision for the graphic design of the journal could not have been realized without the advice of RLS.[31] *m/f* paid for RLS's services through subscriptions and sales.[32]

£1.20   number 1 1978

m/f

a feminist journal

Cover of *m/f: a feminist journal*, 1978, typeset by Red Lion Setters.

Following an earlier period of financial problems, by 1986 RLS was apparently bouncing back.[33] How it responded to desktop publishing, the next technological revolution that shook up typesetting, is not covered in Kitson's book or in other sources. By the early 1990s, with the ANC and SACP no longer outlawed, Norma and David Kitson moved to Zimbabwe. Kitson's obituary writer in the *London Times* suggests that she avoided South Africa, as her political peers there did not recognize her contributions to their causes. Kitson became involved in Zimbabwe Women Writers, where she organized, edited, and wrote.[34]

Red Lion Setters is an example of how the computer-driven feminization of the typesetting profession in the latter half of the twentieth century allowed women to set up their own typesetting businesses and to employ women workers. In the case of RLS, the computerization of typesetting enabled women to contribute to, publicize, and record their political concerns. While the women discussed above would have found a way to do that with or without the typesetting resources of RLS, those resources certainly helped. Nonetheless, the characterization of RLS as a woman-only typesetting collective should be viewed with care. Although sympathetic to feminism and collective working, commitment to these ideals seemed lesser concerns for Kitson; her overriding motivations for creating Red Lion Setters were to provide herself with an independent income and to increase her contribution to the anti-apartheid movement in London.

THE

VVHOLE

BOOKE OFPSALMES

Faithfully

TRANSLATED into ENGLISH

i Metre.

Whereunto is prefixed a discourse declaring not only the lawfulnes, but also
the necessity of the heavenly Ordinance
of singing Scripture Psalmes in
the Churches of
God.

Coll. III.

Let the word of God dwell plenteously in
you, in all wisdome, teaching and exhort-
ing one another in Psalmes, Himnes, and
spirituall Songs, singing to the Lord with
grace in your hearts

Iames. V.

If any be afflicted, let him pray, and if
any be merry let him sing psalmes.

Imprinted
1640

Quick and Correct Compositors at the Case: Early Colonial Women Printers

Sarah McCoy

Much has been written about working women—in particular, their fight for equal pay, the #MeToo movement, the lack of diversity within the workplace, the delicate work-life balance, motherhood, and, most recently, COVID-19's effects on women's careers. A recent web search for "working women and motherhood" brings up an endless list of contemporary articles with ominous titles such as an article in *Forbes* entitled, "The Pressure Is Real for Working Mothers," *The Atlantic*'s "When Women Choose Children over a Career," and Scary Mommy's "2020 Will Be the Death of the Working Mother."[1] All of this makes a woman wonder if all of it is even worth the fight. And, of course, the answer is yes—quickly followed up with the question, "At what cost?"

Bay Psalm Book, 1640, printed in Cambridge, Massachusetts, supervised by Stephen Day (Day's son Matthew may have been responsible for the actual printing). Pages were printed simply and sparsely compared to those of their counterparts in Europe, where more elaborate decorative elements were beginning to appear.

As a working mother of two daughters, and a full-time academic and entrepreneur, I find myself drawn to articles suggesting how to balance my career and home. My days are spent teaching graphic design at a small liberal arts university, moving forward on my scholarly research, and creating design and letterpress work for clients, all the while trying to help my children thrive both in and outside the classroom.

Several years ago, I began to research the lives of early colonial women printers—their work interested me, but so did their situations. Similar to me, they were working women with clients *and* children. I wondered, How did *they* do it all? Their lives were fraught with hardship. It was not uncommon for women to be widowed at a young age by the one person who, in many cases, gave them financial stability and a place within society. These were women with dual roles—they were raising children and working to keep their family businesses afloat. In *Colonial Women of Affairs: A Study of Women in Business and the Professions in America before 1776*, Elizabeth Anthony Dexter discusses the many varied roles of early American women. They ran taverns and were merchants; considered artificers, makers of beautiful bonnets, quilts, and gowns; and "ministering angels" (early healthcare workers), school teachers, land proprietors, actresses, poets, writers, and even printers.[2] Plymouth Colony Governor William Bradford's diary contained this entry about women within the colonies: "The women now wente willingly into the field, and tooke their little-ones with them to set corn."[3] I came to understand that colonial working women shared certain essential characteristics—a willingness to challenge traditional gender roles, complete industriousness, shrewdness in their business dealings, and the ability to be forward-thinking in

Replica of a printing press found in a standard seventeenth-century colonial printshop. Type would have been set by hand in a form, inked by hand, and hand-crank printed.

procuring financial security for themselves and their next generation. All of this sounded similar to traits of many of today's working women.

The colonial printshop was often a family business, started by a father and son. This was also the case during the Incunabula period (from the 1450s until 1500). Johannes Gutenberg's former partner, Johann Fust, and Fust's son-in-law took over Gutenberg's printing business after 1455. There were many and varied roles within the print shop. Men worked as printers, typesetters, type casters, punch cutters, type drafters, and type designers. The idea that women may have filled some of these roles is not entirely without merit. There is considerable lack of scholarship as related to the women discussed in the article. I was unable to find any information about their lives until they were married. In many cases, the woman held a specific role in early printing society or became the sole proprietor of the business after a partner's death. As the sudden death of a spouse resulted in immediate hardship, these women were consumed with securing provisions and maintaining whatever small income they could obtain for daily survival. They faced the seriousness and difficulty of life with intense focus and persever- ance. But historian Richard Demeter's research suggests that "evidence permits a more positive statement about the influence these women exerted in their professional capacity. Without a doubt, if only because of the novelty of the printing press or because of their access to it, all of the nine female printers of the colonial period played a pivotal role in the development of their respective communities."[4]

Elizabeth Glover

Elizabeth (Harris) Glover was the first woman reported to be involved in printing in the United States.[5] Her hardship started even before arriving in America. Glover and her husband, the Reverend Joseph Glover, were from Surrey, England. He was a nonconforming minister who sought new freedom to be able to print religious mate- rials for the new colonies, and so they set out across the Atlantic in July of 1638. Joseph unfortunately died en route, but Elizabeth carried on "bringing with her the first printing press of English America to Massachusetts as part of his estate."[6] With five children by her side, aided by her husband's type compositor, Stephen Daye, Elizabeth Glover successfully set up a press in Cambridge, Massachusetts.[7] Glover's first issued works were a printed broadside and a small almanac entitled *The Freeman's Oath*.[8] Her most ambi- tious and difficult work was a five-by-seven, three-hundred-page rough paraphrase of the Psalms entitled *Bay Psalm Book*.

Glover's print career was cut short by her death at the age of forty-one in August 1643. While the body of her printed work is relatively small, she was able to remain steadfast to her goal of establishing a thriving printshop and laid much of the groundwork for the future Harvard University Press. After her death, her second husband, Henry Dunster (the first president of Harvard University), inherited her printing press, plates, and paper and effectively bridged Glover's pioneering efforts with what was the beginnings of Harvard University Press. This literary foundation was thus laid through perseverance. She forged ahead to a new uncertain land to establish her late husband's dream of setting up a printing company—quite an accomplishment for just one brave woman.

Henry Benbridge, *Elizabeth Ann Timothy*, ca. **1775–85**, **watercolor and gouache on ivory.**

Dinah Nuthead

Dinah Nuthead was one of the best-known early American woman printers. She was based in the Province of Maryland and is believed to have been the first woman to be licensed as a printer in the thirteen colonies.

Nuthead lived in St. Mary's City, where she printed standard legal and clerical government work. She was illiterate, and it is not known whether she understood enough of the printing business to typeset or she employed someone who did. Regardless of her abilities and limitations, she know that she could print commercial and legal forms with relatively little need for literacy and still have steady work. In 1696, Nuthead petitioned the Maryland General Assembly to grant her a license to print all bonds, bills, and warrants of attorney. She paid £100 (today's $20,000) for the license.[9] Her work was neither glamorous nor novel, but she understood the value of specialization within a specific market.

Elizabeth Timothy

Elizabeth Timothy, her husband, Louis, and their four children arrived in Philadelphia in 1731 to set up a "Publick French School."[10] The school was successful. Louis's ability to read and write in multiple languages drew Benjamin Franklin to the Timothy family. In 1733 Franklin and Louis arranged a six-year franchise contract to continue the *South Carolina Gazette*, a weekly newspaper in Charleston, South Carolina.

In 1738, Louis died, leaving one year in his six-year contract with Franklin. Elizabeth Timothy assumed control of the paper and fulfilled the contract's final year. In her new role, she showed steadfastness and an ability to mix motherhood with business; she understood that if she could successfully keep the *Gazette* running, she would have the chance to purchase the paper outright from Franklin in a year and thus provide for her family for the long term. Ever the progenitor of ideas, Timothy, as early as 1746, opened a stationery and book store adjacent to the *Gazette* to further develop her business while staying in close proximity to the original printing house. In 1757, she died. While Timothy enjoyed the privileges of the wife of a prominent and wealthy publisher—a rare situation for women of the time—her association and friendship with Franklin also benefited the family's business development. While these advantages certainly aided Timothy's success, her accomplishment as the first woman in the American colonies to own and publish a newspaper should not be dismissed.

Timothy was able to influence the dissemination of knowledge and to define cultural attitudes and religious thought throughout the early colonies. Her writings and editorials indicate that she was attuned to the interests and tastes of her readers, as she defined and introduced topics to her audience. Timothy sought to maintain an ethical standard in her work by printing information and opinions that would be popular, as well as those intended to be provocative and noteworthy. She and Franklin were both aware of the consequences of printing controversial work but knew that doing so was a virtuous stance worth the risk. Timothy was careful to allow all perspectives in her paper, while she herself remained neutral, thus creating a balanced newspaper and maintaining readership.

Dissemination of Knowledge

These women and other vanguards such Ann Smith Franklin and Sarah Updike Goddard had varied experiences and education (or, in some cases, lack of education), and all underwent hardships.

Nonetheless, their work not only maintained a livelihood for their families, but also gave them a heightened status throughout the early colonies. More importantly, as women, they saw the value of their work in the dissemination of knowledge and the advancement of enlightened thought. All of these women were working when they did not have the guarantee of the Bill of Rights or freedom of speech to protect what they were printing. They promoted literacy and literature in their communities, which eventually led to the American Revolution and redefined the culture of the early United States.

Early printer Margaret Draper of the *Massachusetts Gazette* reminded many of her editorial adversaries of the responsibilities of the press to print contentious ideas, even if they didn't agree with the commonly rising patriot point of view. She faced much opposition and remained unwavering in the face of guaranteed backlash.

In a notice to her readers on her purpose for printing, Sarah Updike Goddard of the *Providence Gazette and Country Journal* wrote:

> But after all our Endeavors to serve and oblige our Benefactors, we, through inadvertency, or Mistake, should err in Judgment, about any particular manner, we hope to be treated with Candor: and trust our general Performance will be thought to merit such Indulgence. For besides a Collection of all the materials and valuable News, both Foreign and Domestic, we shall strive to spread the most useful Knowledge and Instruction; such as will most effectually encourage the Interest in Religion and Virtue; Determination, not to be biased or influenced by Party principles, nor swayed by Bigotry.[11]

These women used their unique understanding of feminine interests to uncover emerging markets for print. For example, on a lighthearted note, the early printer Clementina Rind encouraged her husband, publisher of the *Maryland Gazette*, to print acrostic verses for young couples in honor of Valentine's Day. These poems struck a chord among readers and caused a stir in readership, resulting in more advertising dollars—a shrewd business move, indeed.

I can't help but turn my thoughts to the inclusion of these pioneering women's children in their work. This inclusion was out of necessity, but it was forward-thinking to advance their specific skill sets in the marketplace, fostering their children's economic and societal success. The work of Ann Smith Franklin, editor of the *Rhode Island Gazette*, was carried on after her death by her son, James Jr., who ran the operation of the presses, and daughters Mary and Elizabeth, who performed typesetting. It was said that her daughters "were correct and quick compositors at the case; sensible and amiable women."[12]

Sarah Updike Goddard's influence wasn't finished at her death in 1770; her daughter, Mary Katherine Goddard, went on to become Baltimore's first postmaster in 1775. At the time, her post office was the busiest in the nation. Mary eventually found fame for publishing the first certified copy of the Declaration of Independence in January 1777. But like many women, both past and present, she was challenged in her position by men, based on her gender. In 1789, she was removed from her postmaster position and a man was put in her place. The National Archives contains a letter written by Mary Goddard to George Washington on December 23, 1789, petitioning him to reinstate her, as there were no legitimate grievances against her other than her sex.[13]

While this essay focuses on the virtuous qualities and strong entrepreneurial sense of these early colonial women, there were, I am confident, unrecorded moments of grave difficulty and the boring, unglamorous grind of daily production and business dealings. On top of this, there was the daily necessity of raising a family—many times as a single parent.

"Finding balance" is of contemporary interest, but it isn't easily achieved. Colonial women didn't have the luxury of looking for balance but rather acted out of the necessity for survival. I too find myself caught among the various demands of business, teaching, and motherhood; I'm lucky that I have a more egalitarian partnership that permits me to take on these roles. I look at the characteristics of these early trailblazers with awe and, with that, begin to shift my own attitudes toward an approach that demonstrates for the women in my life perseverance, strong entrepreneurial efforts, charity toward others, and an overarching engagement in contemporary culture.

Dora Pritchett, Dora Laing, Patricia Saunders: The Invisible Women of Monotype's Type Drawing Office

Alice Savoie & Fiona Ross

Bembo, Times New Roman, Gill Sans, Centaur—these are just some of the finest typefaces of the twentieth century that were produced by the Monotype Corporation in the United Kingdom. Each of them is held as a masterpiece of typographic history and is usually associated with the name of its (often male) designer. Very few people realize, however, that typefaces have hardly ever sprung from the genius mind of a lone artist but have historically been the result of a complex set of creative and manufacturing operations involving multiple people and skills. At the heart of the production process behind these Monotype typefaces lay its Type Drawing Office (TDO) and the women who populated it.

Type drawing offices can broadly be identified as internal departments that operated within type foundries or type manufacturing companies. At Monotype, the main role of the TDO from its inception was to create the letter drawings used to produce hot-metal typefaces. TDO employees would adapt a designer's original drawings to a format suitable for the industrial production of matrices or would convert

A drawing clerk tracing the contours of a projected image of Eric Gill's original drawings for Perpetua italic, 1956.

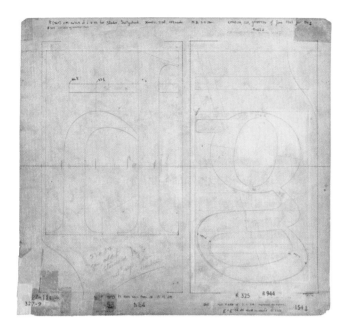

existing typefaces to either hot metal or, by the second half of the twentieth century, phototypesetting or digital type technologies. The TDO also

Reversed 10-inch drawing by Dora Pritchett for letterforms g and h of Monotype Times New Roman, 1931.

expanded character sets and extended the design of typefaces to include variants (such as bold, italic, and condensed) and additional point sizes. The core of the work carried out by the department thus involved turning an original type design idea into a fully working typeface, often in a range of styles and sizes, through an essentially iterative process. These tasks were not confined to Latin script, as Monotype (and other type-manufacturing companies, such as its main competitor, Linotype) produced a number of prominent type-faces for the West Asian, South Asian, and Southeast Asian markets.

Recruitment

The formal setup of the Monotype TDO can be traced back to 1910. At that time, the department was supervised by the works man-ager, Frank Hinman Pierpont, and the head of the TDO, Fritz Max Steltzer. Pierpont and Steltzer typically recruited young women aged sixteen to eighteen who lived near the Monotype plant (located halfway between London and Brighton in the south of England).

Dora Laing at the drawing board in the Monotype TDO, in Salfords, Surrey, UK, probably during the mid-1950s.

Little information survives regarding the profile of TDO members in the first half of the twentieth century; however, we do know that the majority of the women recruited in the postwar era were educated at the local grammar school. Hired as "drawing clerks," they usually took on paid work for a brief period of time after completing their studies and before starting a family. Some drawing clerks, however, stayed in the Drawing Office for many years. Dora Pritchett and Dora Laing, for instance, are two early TDO members who spent their working lives at Monotype and left a long-lasting mark on their colleagues. They played a crucial role in accumulating knowledge and passing it on to a younger generation of TDO employees.

Research findings indicate that Monotype's motivation for hiring young female staff was essentially financial, as women received lower wages than men—a trend that was widely shared in the industrial sector throughout the twentieth century. While photographs and archival material suggest that the TDO employed almost exclusively women drawing clerks until the Second World War, the department increased its intake of male employees from the 1950s onward. By the 1980s, it had achieved an even gender balance.

Skills

The women employed to work in the TDO needed to be meticulous and skilled in their work. They had to be good at arithmetic, have a logical mind, be precise at drawing, and demonstrate an acute sense of letterform proportions. Depending on their abilities and experience, employees could be allocated to one of four sections of the TDO, whose work entailed:

- receiving customer orders and devising matrix-case arrangements;
- charting the dimensions and measurements to be used in the production of each typeface;
- drawing the letterforms in reverse on white card, at a size of 10 inches;
- cutting the wax patterns to be later used in the production of matrices.

Each of these four sections was traditionally supervised by a TDO member. Even though management positions remained a male privilege at Monotype, some women did occupy supervisory roles. Hence, by 1950, Beryl Morris headed the orders and matrix-case section; Emily MacMurray oversaw the charting work; Dora Laing supervised the drawing activities; and Winifred Pooley was responsible for cutting wax patterns.

The TDO was not usually credited for its extensive work on typefaces. In a rare acknowledgment, Monotype praised the skills of the department in a 1956 article published in its house publication, the *Monotype Recorder*:

The tracings are re-drawn in the Type Drawing Office, after much study and the use of critical imagination, by straight-edge and "french curve", this time with a most perceptive effort to interpret and to realize the designer's true intention that each letter should be a consistent "member" of its alphabet....This work of the Type Drawing Office calls not only for very accurate measurement but also for a certain exercise of judgment—and a great deal of accumulated knowledge of type behaviour and the habits of the reading eye. Here the calculations are made, by which a design is subtly adapted to look as right in 12 point as it looks in 8 point. Here, extraneous sorts are designed as required, in harmony with the fount. Measurements are recorded in tenths of a

Patricia Saunders handling the enlargement camera of the Monotype TDO, 1955.

thousandth of an inch, for when the "ten-inch drawings", as they are called, finally go forward to the wax-cutting pantograph, the design stage is closed. Everything thereafter is mechanical work. Up to this point, all the effort, research and experiment has gone to making sure that the design is a good one: readable…, combinable, consistent.

The article is illustrated with illuminating photographs of the TDO and the matrix factory, showing women of all ages (alongside some men) handling the various operations required to produce Monotype faces.

Despite their required skills, drawing clerks were not encouraged to grow their typographic knowledge. According to the late Patricia Saunders (1933–2019), a long-standing Monotype employee: "We were not encouraged to know names or history of fonts; it was

Monotype®

Every new TYPEFACE *has some link with the past as well as bringing fresh hope for the future. The idea of creating Monotype Columbus was sparked off by the opportunity to celebrate the quincentenary of the voyage on which Christopher Columbus made sail from Spanish shores in 1492. The influence of Spain in sponsoring the adventurous voyage made by Columbus was only one of two reasons for deciding to give Spanish flavour to our new type series; the 1992 Olympics also took place on Spanish soil. Therefore Monotype Columbus draws inspiration from types used in Spain to create new text types of economical yet highly readable proportions, and with particularly handsome large display sizes, specifically to meet the requirements of digital typography. The types came from elsewhere in Europe, but the Spanish printers imparted a national style which is reflected in the new typeface. Like the bold man after whom it is named,* MONOTYPE COLUMBUS *sets out with great hopes and powerful support.*

ONOTYPE COLUMBUS has been designed by Patricia Saunders. In 1951 she joined the Monotype Type Drawing Office, where she worked on adapting Jan van Krimpen's Spectrum typeface for Monotype composition, and also on producing John Peters's Castellar titling. She has been involved in making several adaptations of classic revival typefaces such as Bell, Centaur, Felix Titling, Walbaum, and Van Dijck for digital typesetting. Types used in Spain were used merely as a basis from which the roman and italic of Monotype Columbus have been derived. A fresh and lively hand-drawn typeface has been made to suit twentieth-century tastes and needs, retaining a few pleasingly archaic letters such as '*h*', but avoiding other quirky forms which might jar present-day readers. Instead of making a facsimile of a typically irregular fifteenth-century roman and of a sixteenth-century italic, Patricia Saunders has applied her broad experience and highly developed skill and judgement in creating a **beautiful and versatile** new typeface for her contemporaries.

Monotype
Typography Ltd
Perrywood Park
Salfords
Redhill
Surrey RH1 5JP
England
Tel: 0737 765959
Fax: 0737 769243

Monotype
Typography Inc
Suite 504
53 West Jackson
Boulevard
Chicago
Illinois 60604
USA
Tel: 312 855 1440
1-800 MONOTYPE
Fax: 312 939 0378

18 point italic, with semi bold italic   11 point Columbus, with semi bold   8 point semi bold

all [Monotype series] numbers." Yet according to Patricia's husband, David Saunders, who helped supervise some of the TDO's operations in the 1960s and '70s, "Many operations in the TDO were [more] akin to research and development than to straightforward production. Furthermore, although much of the work involved adapting the design of others to suit particular technologies, there was also a considerable creative element."

Type specimen for the typeface Columbus by Patricia Saunders, 1992.

Experience and dedication to the work carried out by the TDO enabled a number of employees to develop valuable skills and, in Patricia's case, to eventually become a credited typeface designer creating new typefaces.

From Drawing Clerk to Type Designer

Patricia Saunders is an inspiring case of a drawing clerk who fought for her career options. Born Patricia Mullett, she was educated at Reigate County School for Girls; after a two-year spell working in an art bookshop, she joined the Monotype TDO in 1951. Trained as a drawing clerk, Patricia contributed to the development of many Monotype faces, such as Castellar, Spectrum, and Glint Ornaments. Like most of her colleagues, her work during the 1950s involved completing character sets for hot-metal typefaces, including drawing optical sizes and developing weight and width variants for existing designs.

Patricia met her husband, David, in the TDO, and after marrying him in October 1959, she left Monotype to start a family the following year. While the majority of young women did not return after having children, Patricia rejoined the company in 1982. By then, the level of skills within the TDO had deteriorated, as she describes:

I went back as a drawing clerk. I was horrified by the lack of skill and knowledge which relied on one person correcting all the work....I was resented and bullied by one member of staff, because I'd had all the experience of earlier times, and I was paid less than some of the less competent people, and also being asked to correct others' bad work....I finally protested [about] my pay and status and it was rectified a bit late.

Saunders had left Monotype when its main activity still revolved around hot-metal typesetting; upon her return, she was asked to adapt and develop typefaces for the Monotype Lasercomp, the industry's first digital laser phototypesetter. Under the supervision of Robin Nicholas, who headed the TDO in the 1980s, she worked to adapt Monotype's renowned existing typefaces, including Van Dijck and Centaur, as well as to completely redesign Felix Titling, which was produced by Monotype in the 1930s and was based on the work of the fifteenth-century calligrapher Felice Feliciano. Saunders is more specifically remembered for her contribution to a series of typefaces produced by Monotype and adopted by Microsoft as their core fonts in the 1980s. Most notably, these include Arial, which was based on Monotype Grotesque and was jointly developed with Robin Nicholas, and the script face Corsiva. In 1992, she designed Columbus, a digital typeface "with a Spanish flavour," as a tribute to the explorer Christopher Columbus. In the type specimen published by Monotype to promote the new design, remarkably, Saunders was not only publicly credited as the designer, but she was also praised for having "applied her broad experience and highly developed skill and judgment in creating a beautiful and versatile new typeface for her contemporaries."

Saunders's career remains exceptional, as most of the women who joined the TDO as drawing clerks left the company without an opportunity to build a prominent career in typography. Yet her example shows that in a more amenable environment, some of these women may have had greater chances to develop their skills, move up the career ladder, and even originate new type designs.

Acknowledging Women's Role in Type History

The drawing clerks of the Monotype TDO were not alone in working anonymously on successful typefaces. Our research suggests that a number of type manufacturers in Europe (such as Deberny & Peignot in France, Simoncini in Italy, and Linotype in the United Kingdom) employed women who actively contributed to the design, development, and production of many typefaces throughout the twentieth century. Such contributions have proved difficult to document, as many of these workers entered the type industry only for a few years before moving on, either to have a family or to take on other (often non-type-related) employment. It has been disheartening to find that many of the women we have managed to trace do not recognize the value of their contributions and do not see the point in reflecting on their experiences. This attitude may partially explain the invisibility of women in current narratives of design history. As Martha Scotford, professor of graphic design, stated:

> For the contributions of women in graphic design to be discovered and understood, their different experiences and roles within the patriarchal and capitalist framework they share with men, and their choices and experiences within a female framework, must be acknowledged and explored.

Twenty-six years after Martha Scotford's plea, much work remains to be undertaken to revise the design canon in relation to typeface design and to ensure that women are accorded the status they deserve.

Acknowledgments

This text was written as part of the research project *Women in Type, a Social History of Women's Role in Type Drawing Offices*, hosted by the University of Reading and funded by the Leverhulme Trust. The authors are grateful to colleague Dr. Helena Lekka for her help on this research. Many thanks to Monotype and Richard Cooper for allowing us to reproduce the documents shown in this article. Thanks to former Monotype employees Duncan Avery, Richard Cooper, Maureen Mitchell, Robin Nicholas, Ann Pillar, Kumar Parminder Rajput, Patricia and David Saunders, Graham Sheppard, and Valerie Wise for taking the time to share their memories with us.

Press On!
Feminist Historiography
of Print Culture and
Collective Organizing

MMS (Maryam Fanni, Matilda
Flodmark, & Sara Kaaman)

"Ever since the days of Mrs. Gutenberg, women have been involved in the art of printing."[1]

So begins the partly satirical anthology *Bookmaking on the Distaff Side* from 1937. In writing book history from the perspective of Johannes Gutenberg's wife, the authors wanted to point out how conventional history writing is based on patriarchal narratives and that such an understanding of history erases an infinite number of women from history books. To address this erasure, members of a loosely formed group of women calling themselves the Distaff Side made an open call for contributions from women in the North American printing industry. About twenty professionals—bookbinders, printers, typographers, illustrators, and authors—

(Top) Workers at the printing house Statlanders in Stockholm, Sweden, 1904. (Bottom) Members of the Women's Typographic Association (Typografiska Kvinnoklubben), 1925. Front row, from left: Ellen Kjellström, Hanna Berg, Augusta Brehmer, Elin Johansson, Hilda Svensson. Center row: Elvira Asmundson, Gerda Jonasson, Lisa Rylander, Astrid Pettersson, Titania Ek, Augusta Löfstedt, Pamela Graf. Top row: Edit Svensson, Josefina Bernström, Hildur Samuelsson.

addressed gender inequalities in the printing industry and print historiography through historical, humorous, and critical essays, poems, manifestos, typographic experiments, and illustrations. The resulting beautifully crafted volume has been described by book historian Kathleen Walkup as a "pot-luck offering."[2]

Workers at the printing house Nymans in Stockholm, Sweden, 1907.

Jane Grabhorn, one of the members of the Distaff Side, organized the publication of the book. She ran with her husband and brother-in-law the acclaimed fine-printing establishment Grabhorn Press in San Francisco. Alongside the family business, she managed her own playful and experimental Jumbo Press. In her satirical contribution to *Bookmaking on the Distaff Side*, entitled "A Typographic Discourse for the Distaff Side of Printing, a Book by Ladies," Grabhorn comments on male dominance in typography:

> Mad, abandoned, the Jumbo Press is revolutionizing the printing world, turning it upside down and topsy turvy, exposing all its hoodoo-voodoo, and divesting its weird ceremonies of all their glamour. Jumbo stripped the mask from typography's Medicine Men and their disciples have seen them as they are: pompous tottering pretenders, mouthing conceits and sweating decadence.[3]

Grabhorn here seeks to expose the exaggerated mystification of the typography trade. However, she uses racialized stereotypes in referring to the printing world as "hoodoo-voodoo" and typographers as "Medicine Men," reflecting her position as a White woman in the 1930s United States.

In her seminal 1994 essay "Messy History vs. Neat History," design historian Martha Scotford describes historiographic mechanisms that exclude women from conventional graphic design history, drawing from art and design historians Cheryl Buckley, Griselda Pollock, and Linda Nochlin.[4] Scotford argues that patriarchal and capitalist logics support and produce a male canon as they concentrate on individuals and individual effort, institutions and businesses, and normative notions of innovation and influence. She goes on to present a typology of positions that often fall outside history books—for example, female spouses or widows who run businesses under their husbands' names.

Inspired by Scotford's concept of messy history, we here consider examples of feminist organizing among printers and typographers from Sweden and the United Kingdom. We do so to see what we can learn from this history and to examine how contemporary understandings of professional identities are constructed.

There is a common misunderstanding that women have been absent from the graphic industry—printing, bookbinding, typesetting—until recently. In fact, female printers existed in the sixteenth century, when the trade was brand new.[5] When the guild system was subsequently introduced, women lost their positions and men held the sole right to the profession. By the end of the 1800s, the situation started to change, and "a struggle between women and men began."[6]

Women in the graphic industry have encountered unique obstacles along the way to being considered equal to their male colleagues. Print workers were among the first occupational groups to organize in trade unions. Printers and typographers had the advantage of direct access to tools for the dissemination of messages, and the Swedish Association for Typographers (Svenska typografförbundet) was founded in Stockholm in 1846.[7] In an anniversary book celebrating the eighty-year history of the association, the Swedish journalist and typographer Nils Wessel wrote:

> It was not with a sense of joy that typographers saw women enter into the printing profession. Their professional pride rose up against the fact that women entered a profession which, more than others, was considered to be reserved for men....However, a day came when women asked to be accepted as members of the Swedish Association for Typographers. The first attack was made at the meeting of the Swedish Association for Typographers on March 7, 1874.[8]

It would take another fourteen years before the association welcomed female members, and despite their inclusion in 1888, it soon became clear that there was a need for female typographers to form their own organization. In 1904, the Women's Typographic Association (Typografiska Kvinnoklubben) was established.

One of the main struggles of the Women's Typographic Association concerned the right to work night shifts. In 1906, Sweden signed an international convention on "protection against the danger of work," which included a ban on women working during the night. Since a large part of typesetting work was done during night shifts, the Women's Typographic Association realized that this law would force many women out of the comparatively well-paid typesetting profession. Along with other women's organizations, the association campaigned against the law, which led to its downfall in the Swedish Parliament in 1908. However, the law was proposed again and won the approval of Parliament, coming into force in 1911.[9]

Another struggle that the Women's Typographic Association waged was against the notion that women were by nature inferior typographers. In 1931, an article was published in the daily newspaper *Dagens Nyheter* with the headline "The Suffragettes Have Not Won the Government. Women Are Bad as Typographers. Exceptional Physical Qualities Necessitate Protection." In the article, typographer and printing-house owner Hugo Lagerström argued that women's work did not give proper results, partly because women had difficulty standing up: "The same [inferiority] applies to girls as loaders, it is a heavy job for which women have only been used temporarily. In general, their performance will never be such that it can compete with men's."[10]

Elin Johansson represented the Women's Typographic Association in replying to Lagerström's sexist stereotypes, highlighting the often invisible double workload that was (and still is) the everyday life of many working women:

> The headline alone, "Women Are Bad as Typographers," makes a rather depressing impression…especially as there are large printing houses in Stockholm that have had only female labor for many years. It would have been better if the managers of these printing houses had commented on the female workforce….To claim that we belong to the weaker sex is a bit ridiculous. By the end of the workday, many of us also have the home to take care of, perhaps for several hours, while the man only has to sit down at a set table.[11]

Historically, wage policy has been based on the idea that society is made up of heterosexual nuclear families with a male breadwinner. The reality has always been different for many women. Historians Ulla Wikander and Inger Humlesjö both argue that the trade union movement made the mistake of building its struggle on male breadwinners.[12] Women were perceived as a threat to their male colleagues for several reasons. They were paid less and could thus be targeted for wage dumping, the practice of employers offering wages much lower than the standard in an industry. Women were also preferred by employers because they tended to be more sober than their male colleagues. Wikander writes, "Typographer struggles are of great interest for anybody who wants to understand both the limited participation of women in unions, and men's attitudes to women also after they had joined."[13]

The tensions between male and female labor forces in the field of printing and typography, which were sparked by industrialization and new machinery in the late 1800s, are mirrored by the radical shifts that followed the computerization of printing and typography through the advent of phototypesetting processes in the 1970s. Machines moved from hot-metal type to "cold" photographic film processes and, perhaps more importantly, to a QWERTY keyboard similar to that of a typewriter. The former print worker and union activist Megan Dobney, now regional secretary of the Trades Union Congress in London, explains,

> Before it had been about "we men with our heavy metal" and the "girls out there typing." But, when the technology changed, typesetting was being done on QWERTY keyboard rather than old linotype keyboard. Typesetting became typing rather than putting 26 lead soldiers together. And in Britain by the 1970s it was women who were typists, not men, so if there was an opening for a typist it would be a woman who went for it, generally speaking. What was happening of course was that girls typing don't cost that much when compared to men with five years of apprenticeships, so there was a concern that the jobs would start drifting into the non-union sector.[14]

Dobney's testimony shows how technological changes can instigate gendered conflicts in the workplace but can also provide women the opportunity to enter into and be recognized in new professional roles.

While the commercial printing industry was undergoing vast changes, as witnessed by Dobney, liberatory and activist movements across the world were gaining direct access to printing as a tool for disseminating their ideas through the establishment of small-scale, radical presses. As Jess Baines has shown through her extensive research, printed flyers, posters, magazines, books, and pamphlets were important tools in feminist collective organizing for their opportunities to build new discourses and new languages. Baines writes,

> "Women's Lib" was frequently ridiculed or reviled in the larger culture, sentiments reflected in the printing trade. Printing was also expensive. The second-hand or loaned stencil-duplicator served a mighty role in this breach, but its capabilities were limited in terms of quantity, quality and format. The women's movement needed a press, or better still presses, of [its] own.[15]

In this way, the twentieth-century women's liberation movement rediscovered the concept of the "private press," known since the late nineteenth century as a tool for distributing dissident content.[16]

The construction of today's graphic designer identity can be traced to historical shifts and changes within the printing industry. While feminist activism was pressing on "in the margins" in the 1980s and thereafter, two neoliberal political trends deeply affected professional identification within printing, typography, and beyond, leading to a more individualistic professional subject without connections to the labor movement.

First, in step with digitalization, traditionally strong graphic unions became increasingly weakened. An internationally significant example is the failure of the year-long print worker's strike in the Wapping district of London in 1986. The strike came after the media mogul Rupert Murdoch fired six thousand newspaper printers and replaced them with secretly trained electricians, who took over the work at a new printing plant. This, together with the defeat of the British mining strike the previous year, were steps in the Margaret Thatcher regime's dismantling of labor laws and trade union organization, the effects of which are still seen today.

Second, as the British cultural theorist Angela McRobbie has proposed, the concept of creativity and the identification with and ideal of being creative in one's professional role has served as a political propaganda tool in the United Kingdom.[17] She believes that the so-called creative ideal—which weirdly suggests that some professions are more creative than others—produces an individualist self-employed worker who above all loves to work, regardless of financial compensation and working conditions. McRobbie believes that this ideal worker affects conditions for all jobholders, who are expected to adapt to and behave like this figure. Today, there is a strong narrative—perpetuated through advertising, TV, and social media—that equates freedom with working on your laptop in a café, on your phone on the bus, or just about anywhere. Women and Black and Indigenous People of Color (BIPOCs) are the people most affected by this deterioration in living and working conditions and the demand for flexibility.

The German art group kleines postfordistisches Drama artistically examines and describes the living and working situation of cultural workers today and how these can be understood as a model for politically driven self-entrepreneurship:

> She now works flexibly from home, without external controls. She works when she wants to. However, she has to carry out an incalculable amount of work for a fixed fee. This means that she does nothing but work at home. The route to the desk to read e-mails and answer e-mails at her laptop has become as much of a routine as the way to the kitchen to make coffee. The jobs she is paid for, those done and those not done, are only a small part of what she does every day. Organizing a meeting, doing the washing, learning a new program, preparing dinner, writing invoices, shopping, doing her tax return, booking a flight, keeping up contacts, showing interest—all this becomes too much for her sometimes.[18]

When attempts are made to update historiography to make room for women, individual success stories are often highlighted. This strategy casts a shadow over workers and collectives in favor of individual names. It solidifies the professional identity of the designer as an individual success seeker. But when we look for histories of collectivity and collegiality, beyond elevated names, a different picture emerges—one that might help us arrive at new understandings of how professional roles and identities today are constructed, and the struggles at hand.

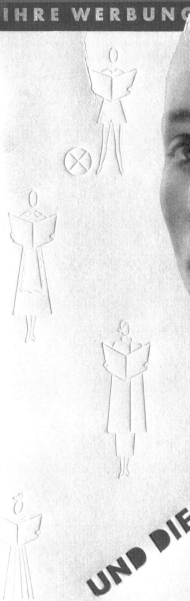

UND DIE FRAU

söre

On Söre Popitz, the Bauhaus's Only Known Woman Advertising Designer

Madeleine Morley

In Germany during the 1930s, there was one lifestyle magazine that every young woman had to have. An essential for those donning flapper skirts, cropped haircuts, and dramatic eyeliner, *Die neue Linie* first appeared on the newsstands in 1929 with a sensational lowercase title on its cover and articles on everything from fashion and home decor to sports. Art directed by former Bauhaus master Herbert Bayer—and featuring work by László Moholy-Nagy and Walter Gropius—the stylish women's monthly was as modern as it came. Working on the magazine alongside those celebrated men of modernism was one lesser-known designer: she went by the name of Söre Popitz.

Born Irmgard Sörensen in 1896, Popitz is the only woman known to have pursued a career in graphics after studying at the Bauhaus. The designer and artist passed away in 1993 at ninety-seven; her life encompassed nearly the entirety of the twentieth century. When she first began freelancing in the 1920s, it was almost unheard of for a woman to work in advertising design and art

Söre Popitz, *Ihre Werbung und die Frau*, advertising brochure for the publisher Otto Beyer, Leipzig, Germany, 1934, cardboard, silver leaf, letterpress printing on paper.

direction. Through a unique set of circumstances, Popitz slipped through a crack and into the field of commercial arts, learning her craft from the originators of German modernism and going on to pursue her own career.

When Popitz enrolled as a student at the Weimar Bauhaus in October 1924, she'd just completed seven years of training at the prestigious Academy of Fine Arts in Leipzig. There, she had studied under the seminal modernist type designer Jan Tschichold and was one of only a handful of women permitted into the school. By the time she had moved on to the Bauhaus, that school had progressively allowed women into the classroom, though women were encouraged to pursue weaving rather than the male-dominated mediums of painting, architecture, and typography.[1] Popitz enrolled with the hope of meeting kindred spirits and participated in the school's first-year preliminary course, taught by Moholy-Nagy and Josef Albers. She left after only two semesters, never reaching the point in the curriculum where she would likely have been ushered away from graphics and into the weaving workshop.

It was because of this early turn of events that Popitz was ultimately able to succeed in an industry where other women struggled to get a foot in the door. It's not completely clear why Popitz didn't continue studying at the Bauhaus when the school moved from Weimar to Dessau at the end of her second semester. Reading between the lines of her diary, held at the Bauhaus Dessau Foundation archive, it seems likely that she didn't align herself with the school's new motto: "art and technology—a new unity." Nevertheless, when Popitz moved back to Leipzig to set out on her own, she brought her Bauhaus training to commissions for publishers, household appliance companies, and other local businesses. Although many of her commercial designs bear the unmistakable influence of her male modernist mentors, Popitz embellished her work with blocky characters that represented a range of female experiences, lending her designs a distinctively feminine sensibility.

"Since I Could Think": Söre Popitz's Early Years

It was Popitz's grandmother who first inspired her to pick up a paintbrush, according to the designer's diary. "I am often asked, 'Since when have you painted?' Answer: 'Since I could think!'" she writes, going on to describe her painted illustrations for her grandmother's folktales.[2] As a teenager in Kiel, Germany, Popitz attended the city's craft college. Then in 1917 she decided to fully commit to a career in advertising draftsmanship and moved to Leipzig to attend the Academy of Fine Arts. A class photograph from the time shows her and a few other women peeking out from a dense hedge of suits.

According to Steffen Schröter, a Bauhaus Dessau Foundation staffer who researched Popitz's estate, Academy of Fine Arts professor and graphic artist Hugo Steiner-Prag was responsible for opening the academy's enrollment to women.[3] Steiner-Prag's stance, however, was heavily disputed by his colleagues, and it took Popitz two application cycles to receive a placement.

Once Popitz had finally enrolled, her work quickly caught the attention of the local design community. Her designs were displayed in an exhibition of advertising art, and in 1920 she won a prominent poster competition. The style of her pieces was in keeping with the period's decorative, flamboyant illustration, though Popitz's figures reveal a level of abstraction, pointing toward the stripped-backed, linear aesthetic that she would later embrace along with her fellow Bauhauslers.

During her studies at the academy, Popitz became acquainted with Tschichold and sat in on his lectures. Art historian Patrick Rössler notes the pivotal influence of the 1923 Weimar Bauhaus exhibition on the young designer: visiting the show in person, Popitz was apparently struck in particular by Moholy-Nagy's typographic work, furthering her initiation into modernism.[4] When she graduated from the academy in 1924, she married the Leipzig-based physician and anthroposophist Friedrich Popitz. But her curiosity about modern design had been piqued, and she became increasingly interested in the Bauhaus as its reputation for experimental design pedagogy continued to grow. Popitz set off to Weimar to find out more. "I went to the Bauhaus because I was keen to meet like-minded people," she wrote in her diary.[5]

Material Sculptures: Student Life at the Bauhaus

All students at the Bauhaus received a year of basic training as part of their preliminary course, during which they experimented with color, shape, and materials. While Popitz was a student in Weimar, the course was team-taught by Moholy-Nagy and Albers. Moholy-Nagy focused on construction, balance, and materials, while Albers taught craft techniques. During one of Moholy-Nagy's workshops on balance and the visual principles, Popitz created a study from glass, wire, metal, and wood, structured so that two black cubes and a white beam appear to float in space. A few years later, Moholy-Nagy published a photograph of her piece in his seminal book, *From Material to Architecture*, and it subsequently became an iconic example of the school's pedagogy.[6]

In her diary, Popitz writes only briefly about her time studying under Moholy-Nagy: "Yesterday I had to complete what Moholy buried us in. He wants the highest aim to be the mathematical calculation of form. For example, balance is calculated mathematically by so much red, so much blue, so much yellow....Art and mathematics must become one and the same, uniting in such a way that there is no 'art per se' any more. This has given me something to think about."[7]

Tellingly, she concludes her diary entry with the declaration that she doesn't have to busy herself with this philosophical question about the new direction of art because "no woman can have anything to do with art."[8] Her statement reveals the patriarchal stranglehold still dissuading women from intellectual and artistic pursuits, despite the increasingly inclusive politics of the more progressive schools.[9]

As part of the preliminary course at the Bauhaus, students attended color theory lectures by Paul Klee and Wassily Kandinsky. Popitz's abstract paintings during her time in Weimar—and also later in her life—bear the unmistakable influence of Klee's artistic sensibility.

"The lessons with Klee, the color seminar with Kandinsky, and the material sculptures with Moholy-Nagy were all very important to me. But I could not join in with the Bauhaus' next developments," she wrote cryptically in her diary.[10]

Designing New Lines: Freelancing in Leipzig

On returning to Leipzig in 1926, Popitz printed business cards that described herself as a specialist in "advertising design." One early commission was an ad for a local gymnastics studio run by her close friend Charlotte Selver. The poster's concise lettering on a clear, geometric grid seems to splice together a Tschicholdian approach to typography with the forms used by Moholy-Nagy and Bayer for Bauhaus communications.

It's especially clear how formative Popitz's brief time at the Bauhaus had been when looking at the stripped-back, linear ads she produced for a household appliance company named Thügina. Popitz's series depicts different figures standing beside Thügina's sinks and stoves—a stick-figure doctor, a husband and wife, a group of girls. Further ads feature a range of different types of women, from young girls in patterned dresses to housewives in aprons and

Söre Popitz, advertisement for Thügina, ca. 1925–33.

lean figures dressed in stylish frocks, feathered hats, and glamorous earrings.

These playful, geometric stick figures recall the costumes in Bauhaus professor Oskar Schlemmer's *Triadic Ballet*. The household appliances on each poster are drawn in elegant, thin black lines and lack detailing, which, along with the unfussy typography, communicate cleanliness and efficiency. Everything about these designs would have conveyed modernity, functionality, and simplicity—ideal for modern consumers with their newly electronic, gas-heated, fully-functioning apartments. And Popitz's stylish stick women, rendered abstractly, ranged

die neue linie

AUGUST 1931

heft 12 august 1931 preis 1 mark verlag otto beyer leipzig / berlin

from the traditional to the modern, appealing to housewives and working women alike.

Söre Popitz, title page of the magazine *Die neue Linie*, issue 12, August 1931.

As a freelancer, Popitz worked with the Leipzig publishing house Otto Beyer, which published *Die neue Linie*—a collaboration she would continue for twenty years. One of her most technically impressive designs for the publisher was a 1935 advertising brochure that places a woman's face amid a field of embossed figures;

On Söre Popitz, the Bauhaus's Only Known Woman Advertising Designer her use of photomontage mirrors Moholy-Nagy's. (Popitz likely experimented with the technique as a student in the Bauhaus's preliminary course.) It's a sophisticated piece of design, employing silver foil, die-cut letters, and delicate embossing onto its light paper. As in her Thügina ads, each delicately rendered female figure is dressed in a different outfit, from an apron to a schoolgirl's skirt to a fashionable evening dress. What all the figures have in common is the large publication that they hold open in their hands. With the design, Popitz suggests that all women can read and see themselves in Otto Beyer. The multiplicity of her figures attempted to reach not an everywoman, but every woman.

It was through working with Otto Beyer and her acquaintance with Herbert Bayer that Popitz advised on the relaunch of the firm's flagship women's magazine under the name *Die neue Linie*, which translates to "the new line."[11] The cover of its first issue featured a photomontage by Moholy-Nagy depicting a woman in a fur coat looking out of a large, glass lattice window toward a mountain range. Moholy-Nagy's cover linked the modern architecture of the times—with its emphasis on dramatic glass windows—to the style of the new, modern woman. The "new line" of the magazine's name referred to modern design as much as it did to the new female silhouette. As Patrick Rössler reports, Popitz likely put Otto Beyer in contact with her former teacher for the commission.[12]

Popitz's own commissions for the magazine ranged from illustrations and collages to the design of the back cover, as well as advertising pages in which type treatments are merged with tiny spot drawings. She created just one front cover for *Die neue Linie*, in August 1931, and her photomontage clearly gestures back to Moholy-Nagy's inaugural cover in its use of a mountain range background. In front of a landscape of snow-topped peaks, an illustrated woman with stylish cropped hair and a cap stands on a platform. This balcony, with its three thin, horizontal poles against a white wall, instantly recalls the design of the balconies lining the white-walled student dorms of the Bauhaus building in Dessau, which Popitz had visited a few years prior. The inclusion of this distinctly modern architectural detailing was especially fitting for the issue, as it featured an article by the Bauhaus's first director and Dessau building architect, Walter Gropius.

BODE
GYMNASTIK
HARMONISCHE UND RHYTHMISCHE KÖRPERERZIEHUNG

CHARLOTTE
SELVER-WITTGENSTEIN

NEUE KURSE   DIPL·LEHRERIN DER BODEGYMNASTIK MITGL·DES DEUTSCHEN GYMNASTIKBUNDES

KINDER·MÄDCHEN
FRAUEN · MÄNNER

SONDERKURSE FÜR ÄLTERE DAMEN

AUSKUNFT UND ANMELDUNG
THOMASGASSE 4 IV FAHRSTUHL
SPRECHZEIT MONTAG BIS DONNERSTAG 6–½8

EINTRITT JEDERZEIT

Real Pictures: The War and Postwar Years

Söre Popitz, *Bode Gymnastik*, 1925–30, poster.

Otto Beyer remained Popitz's sole employer during Germany's National Socialist years. To better tolerate the hardships of wartime life, Popitz turned to decorative painting. She drew flowers, detailed self-portraits, and other politically harmless illustrations, writing in her diary that she lacked any inspiration for "real pictures."

At the beginning of the Nazi regime, Popitz attempted to hide all of her Bauhaus studies in the basement of her husband's medical office, yet they were still destroyed, during the bombing of Leipzig. The majority of her early work was lost, and what exactly she produced for Otto Beyer during the war years remains a mystery, as the publishing house was heavily damaged as well. Steffen Schröter notes that due to all these losses, the true scope of Popitz's commercial output will forever remain unknown.[13]

After the Soviet occupation of East Germany, Söre and Friedrich Popitz fled to Frankfurt am Main. Friedrich died only a few months after their escape. From 1949 onward, Popitz worked as a drafts-person for the Schwabe publishing house, a branch of Otto Beyer, and seems to have stopped pursuing work in advertising. For the next half of her life, her largest body of commercial work was the design of a number of patterns for Insel-Bücherei, a book series where each title is wrapped in an abstract background.

Browsing any secondhand bookstore in Germany today, you'll find piles of the ubiquitous Insel-Bücherei series in dusty corners, and it's within these stacks that you're most likely to come across a design by Popitz. Her patterns from the 1950s and '60s depart from her previous style and feature dense, expressionistic tangles of leaves, wispy brushstrokes, and deep blue waves of solemn paint. What was once modern must have seemed long ago.

———

This article first appeared in AIGA Eye on Design *in March 2019. The author would like to thank her editor, Meg Miller, for her insights, as well as Max Boersma for his input.*

Clearing the Fog: Marget Larsen, San Francisco Designer

Sean Adams and Louise Sandhaus

Mutually intrigued by Marget Larsen and her work, Sean Adams and Louise Sandhaus came together to author this text. Rather than create a seamless biography, Louise's comments appear as a kind of parasite on top, or in the cracks, of Sean's elegant and assured narrative. Louise's comments offer additional historic detail as well as historiographic reflections. The contributions of both Sean and Louise are noted by their bracketed initials.

———

Marget Larsen was one of those luminaries of the mid-century who seemed to design anything—and make it last. Those wonderful Joseph Magnin boxes or the striking logo for The Cannery—they are impossible to date fifty years later. That's great design. It's one thing to create a look that is perfect for the times, but quite another to evoke the same good feelings two generations later.[1]
— Roger Black

Marget Larsen, Christmas wrapping paper for Joseph Magnin department store, 1963.

Marget Larsen, advertisement for Joseph Magnin department store, 1958, illustration by Betty Brader Ashley.

[SA] Louis Danziger introduced Marget Larsen's work to me my first year at the California Institute of the Arts (CalArts). At the time, as students, we were hell-bent on creating "new-wave" design. I recognized her work in the boxes from my mother's shopping at Joseph Magnin and visits for ice cream at Ghirardelli's at The Cannery in San Francisco. But at eighteen, I wanted only to plaster the world with Univers 68 and neon colors.

[LS] In contrast to Sean's four-year graphic design education at CalArts, Larsen's was inconsistent. Her mother was a flatware designer, and her father was a builder, so perhaps there was something in the water at the Larsen home. In any case, formal education in graphic design wasn't offered at the time (the 1940s). Instead, you could study to become an "applied artist." My own father was one of those, but often those who became commercial practitioners had studied fine arts or, like Larsen, had picked it up on their own.

She periodically took classes at what became the San Francisco Art Institute, including a sculpture class with the much-ballyhooed modern artist Robert Boardman Howard and the modernist jewelry designer Margaret De Patta, who had studied with László Moholy-Nagy at "The New Bauhaus," the IIT Institute of Design at Illinois

Institute of Technology in Chicago. Both Howard and De Patta were influenced by the avant-garde, but it may have been De Patta in particular who introduced Larsen to Bauhaus-inspired design and concerned her with social causes.[2] It's anyone's guess how Larsen became familiar with typography, layout, or the processes necessary to produce commercial work, but, as was common at the time, it's likely that she art directed others who had expertise in typography and production. The employer who put her on the map, Cyril Magnin of the Joseph Magnin department store chain, recalled her stately beauty and her natural eye and sense of color, proportion, and harmony.[3] In other words, she had the innate instincts for which no education can train.

[SA] Jennifer Morla, who interviewed for a position with Larsen in 1975, describes Larsen's work: "Marget, like Los Angeles designer Deborah Sussman, could translate her design solutions into monumental signage for building identities. Her massive metal star serves as the identity for The Cannery Building. This is timeless design rather than the otherwise gaudy design for the tourist attraction, Fisherman's Wharf." Richard Coyne, *Communication Arts* magazine founder, said, "Only once in a while, a great talent appears on the scene, someone who creates original, beautiful, classic, joyful and wonderful things. Marget Larsen was one of those people. She was noted for her ability to quickly evaluate work and identify what worked and what didn't."[4]

What we don't have access to, however, is Larsen herself. She died prematurely at sixty-two. And like other great creatives—such as Alvin Lustig, who died at forty in 1955—her work faded from the graphic design canon. Steven Heller introduced Lustig's body of work to a new generation of designers in a 1993 *Eye* magazine piece.[5] In 2009, I wrote about Larsen for *Design Observer*, and in 2014, Louise reintroduced Larsen's work in her book *Earthquakes, Mudslides, Fires & Riots: California and Graphic Design, 1936–1986*.

[LS] Unfortunately, I must fess up here that I credited some work in my book to Larsen that was actually the work of others. Shamefully misidentified was the 1967 ad "It's a leg watcher's year!" in which a yellow-tights-clad leg pins down the bold, abstract red shadow of a joyful figure in the background. Worst of all my mistakes is attributing to Larsen the swash script, typographic Joseph Magnin logo. It's distinctive today and indeed rocked the retail world in its time. The ad was art-directed by Marlon Chapman, featuring a Gail Mitchem illustration. I'll take my deserved lashes (self-inflicted ones included), but it points to the messy construction of history. Mistakes are made, and facts emerge.

In addition to an abundance of laudatory anecdotes about Larsen, a trove of newspaper articles praises her work. From 1954 until the late 1970s, Larsen appeared in the San Francisco press and in newspapers nationally. In 1977, she, with her partner Robert Freeman, redesigned the Santa Rosa newspaper, the *Press Democrat*. The agility of her mind is apparent as she describes her thinking process about the paper's new logo:

> The name [*The*] *Press Democrat* is a very long name. So in order to get strength into it…I had the problem of how I was going to handle such a long name. A three-word name. And I was trying for something else besides the name. I felt if I could also have the name read as symbol or a mark it would be a great advantage. It would be something you would see and you know what those words said—like looking at one word.[6]

For years, the San Francisco Advertising Club bestowed the Marget Larsen Award for design or for art direction. Those who have received it, including Morla, count it among their most cherished honors.

So how and why have Larsen's contributions disappeared from history? And if Larsen has been forgotten and Alvin Lustig has been forgotten (and then there was *Elaine* Lustig, who was forgotten too), how many others are also unknown or forgotten? The history of graphic design is much deeper than we can even begin to imagine.

[SA] To understand Larsen's work, it is necessary to understand San Francisco in the 1960s. As Joan Didion writes in her essay "Slouching Towards Bethlehem":

> **It was not a country in open revolution. It was not a country under enemy siege. It was the United States of America in the cold late spring of 1967, and the market was steady and the G.N.P. high and a great many articulate people seemed to have a sense of high social purpose and it might have been a spring of brave hopes and national promise, but it was not, and more and more people had the uneasy apprehension that it was not. All that seemed clear was that at some point we had aborted ourselves and butchered the job, and because nothing else seemed so relevant I decided to go to San Francisco. San Francisco was where the social hemorrhaging was showing up. San Francisco was where the missing**

(Above) Marget Larsen, environmental graphics for Shandygaff Restaurant, San Francisco, California, 1971. (Below) Marget Larsen, identity and packaging for Parisian Bakerie, 1960, art direction by Robert Freeman and George Dippel.

children were gathering and calling themselves "hippies."[7]

At the end of World War II, thousands of service-people disembarked in San Francisco. Veterans who identified as intellectuals, writers, artists, homosexuals, eccentrics, and just plain oddballs remained in San

Francisco rather than returning to their prewar lives in rural America. It's hard to return to milking cows if you're the strangest person in Saline County, Missouri.

[LS] A San Francisco native, Larsen began her career in post–World War II America before the dramatic cultural shifts of the 1960s. In the early 1950s, the visionary civic leader and department store magnate Cyril Magnin hired Toni Moran as advertising manager at Joseph Magnin (JM)—the hip sibling of the matronly I. Magnin stores. In the early 1960s, the chain became the West Coast source of youthful, sophisticated, and cosmopolitan fashion. Cyril credited Moran as the person who established the visionary reputation and image of the retail venture, in great part by hiring Marget Larsen on the heels of bringing illustrator Betty Brader on board.

At JM, Larsen's talent came to full fruition and received full appreciation. The team of Larsen and Brader worked furiously to produce splashy advertising that represented a spirit of West Coast informality, youth, and newness. It was early days for the use of color in newspapers, but as the excitement about JM grew, Cyril Magnin was willing to spend the extra dollars to garner attention. Magnin recalled Larsen designing accessories when needed for an ad, after which he would find a manufacturer to make the item. Cyril Magnin had balls. Larsen had balls, too.

Magnin, a civic leader and influencer, was a champion of Larsen. In 1964, as San Francisco port authority president, he invited her to review plans for the revitalization of Fisherman's Wharf that were part of an initiative to redevelop the waterfront as a historic district. Although the recommendations that she and maritime enthusiast Karl Kortum developed weren't accepted, the invitation reflects Larsen's growing reputation, authority, and respect.[8]

[SA] Since the mid-1950s, San Francisco's City Lights bookstore had been the center for Beat culture, which evolved during the 1960s into the hippie movement. In contrast to New York, with its establishment advertising's reliance on Swiss Helvetica and crisp photography, San Francisco demanded alternative thinking. Larsen magically combined the psychedelic poster scene and DIY graphics created in garages with high fashion and remarkable craft.

Unlike mainstream advertising's clumsy attempts to co-opt the counterculture movement (Canada Dry Wink's "Join the cola drop-outs" and Dash laundry detergent's "Somebody had to break the rules" with mod model Peggy Moffitt), Larsen's work was personal.[9] Her advertising work at Freeman & Gossage ignored the time's standards: a large photograph, clever headline, explanatory text, and

Marget Larsen for Freeman, Mander & Gossage agency, "Ecology and War," Friends of the Earth advertisement, 1969.

logo in the corner. Instead, she turned to alternative media and formats.

[LS] By the early 1960s, when she may have been still employed by Joseph Magnin or working as an independent contractor, Larsen began to art direct ads for Weiner & Gossage (which later became

Freeman & Gossage and a multitude of other combinations). These ads appeared in national publications for clients including Eagle Shirts, the Whiskey Distillers of Ireland, and the Sierra Club. The ads often resembled editorials, albeit with cheeky copy delivered in confident and authoritative typographic packaging. This sensibility stood out and garnered the work numerous advertising and design awards.

Marget Larsen, Christmas boxes, Joseph Magnin department store, 1963.

[SA] An ad for Friends of the Earth states the group's demands to end the war in Southeast Asia. Rather than relying on a traditional ad layout, Larsen turned to what we would now consider a postmodern approach. A photograph is replaced by an antique etching of warfare. The typeface, Caslon, ignores that period's modernist typographic trend of using a clean sans serif typeface. There is no catchy headline. In fact, the layout refers to and is digested as literature. Cues such as the mix of italic and capital letters, fleur-de-lis ornaments, and symmetrical format reinforce the message's veracity and gravity.

Marget Larsen, parking sign,
Cannery Row, 1967.

Larsen's mastery of typography is consistently evident. Herb Lubalin worked with a similarly eclectic, anti-Helvetica aesthetic in New York, but Larsen retained a distinctly California approach. Again, rejecting the expected direction, her ads for Joseph Magnin are aligned with a West Coast aesthetic of craft and the handmade rather than with glossy high fashion. What is essential to recognize is the radical nature of her solutions. Imagine an environment where all fashion advertising and promotion must include exaggerated, hyperreal, and flawless imagery with the obligatory delicate typeface, Firmin Didot. (Wait, that's today.) Against this backdrop, Larsen's work is bereft of high-end photography in preference to illustration and, in some instances, no imagery.

In Larsen's packaging for JM, she again ignored the conventional by featuring psychedelic color combinations, multiple patterns and typefaces, and unique constructions. It might be easy to dismiss Christmas packaging as frivolous, but Larsen's JM boxes set a benchmark that others attempt to meet today. Her Christmas boxes not only became collectible artifacts but also solved the long-standing problem of the need for a gift-wrapping service at a department store. Now, here is the progressive concept years ahead of its time: traditionally, a brand is created with repeated exposure to the same graphic system and logo. The viewer learns to associate a brand with a specific and consistent visual form. Larsen ignored this. Each year, Larsen designed a new set of boxes, eventually passing the project to JM art director Joe Hong. One year's approach was eclectic typography and intense colors; other years featured boxes that could be used as games or a collection of architecturally themed boxes. The differences became the unifying theme, with Larsen's apparent skill and strong visuals the only constants—a through-line connects this approach to the variable identity systems of the 1980s, such as those of MTV and Nickelodeon.

By no means were Larsen's Christmas boxes the sole inspiration for the Fillmore posters of the 1960s, which were shaped by LSD, open sexual morality, and antiestablishment ideas. The posters promoted music and hallucinogenic experiences, not shopping and consumerism. While Larsen's work was based on her design concepts, many of the Fillmore posters resulted from low-production opportunities. Nevertheless, they shared the intensity of Larsen's colors and her rejection of representational content; designers such as Wes Wilson, Bonnie MacLean, and Victor Moscoso rarely displayed a band's or artist's image on a poster.

Larsen's skill with materiality and form are evident in her packaging for Dean Swift snuff and Parisian bread. The user of Dean Swift unwrapped one gold box followed by another gold box, paisley paper, and tins. The extravagance of artifacts resembles elaborate Victorian ornamentation, and the process of unpacking the product matches the message of the graphics.

On the other end of the ornamental spectrum, Larsen's Parisian bread packaging bluntly pronounces the product name and French heritage with no excess. Larsen, recognizing the potential for a bold message, applied typography and forms that turn the package's tall, narrow shape into an advantage. The result is a billboard displayed in a store or seen on the street. Both the Dean Swift and Parisian projects articulate Larsen's talent with three-dimensional form and understanding of how people interact with an artifact. While other designers decorated bags and boxes, Larsen uniquely integrated design, size, shape, material, and graphics.

Larsen's environmental design work was often interrupted or canceled by the bureaucracy of urban planning committees and decision-makers' groups that had no design experience. But the work that was implemented is sublime. Since The Cannery's opening in 1967, its massive star has been a city landmark, a magnificent use of empty space and architecture. Here parking signs, typically bland, are elaborate and playful toys. These were my first memories of graphic design when I was four, and I was obsessed with redrawing them.

[LS] In 1971, when Sean was only seven, a clever child like he was might have noticed an article in the *San Francisco Examiner* entitled "Super SuperGraphics."[10] Among the many pages of local supergraphics were several typographic ones by Larsen. Her brilliance with scale is seen in the simple painting of a nondescript corner building with enormous, high-contrast letterforms. The Bagel Shop on Bush and Polk Streets featured giant, building-height stencil lettering that wrapped the corner, spelling B-A-G-E-L, transforming the space into a celebration. She wrapped another building—one at 1760 Polk Street, housing a San Francisco "healthy food" hot spot—in bold, condensed, sans serif lettering stretching from sidewalk to rooftop, spelling out "SHANDYGAFF." Her supergraphics went head-to-head with the more notable and recognized ones of Barbara Stauffacher Solomon, although Larsen's were purely typographic.

[SA] Larsen's Thonet cardboard box best typifies her aptitude with form. The box, printed with a graphic of Michael Thonet's Antique No. 4 Café Daum Chair (ca. 1890), combines an industrial and utilitarian material with simple modernist functionality and Victorian gingerbread ornament. Here, Paul Klee's sense of wit and parody interweaves with the 1960s West Coast rejection of Bauhaus International Style. The box displays Larsen's ability to create work in two and three dimensions, merge styles and ideas, express playfulness and joy, and produce a unique solution that is entirely of her own genius.

There are times and places imbued with creative energy and change: Paris at the end of the nineteenth century, Los Angeles in the 1930s, New York in the 1950s, and London in the 1970s. Larsen was a defining figure in San Francisco as the epicenter of change and creativity in the 1960s. Her work embodied the revolutionary zeitgeist of the period in her rejection of the established, experiments with materials and form, and intense color palette that challenged traditions of "good taste." Her work, approach, and legacy are expressed best by lyrics sung by Mama Cass Elliot of a "new world coming…in peace…in joy…in love."

Tuesday   October 25   8:00 p.m.
"The Frame"

Thursday   October 27   8:00 p.m.
"Surrealism and Dada"

Wednesday   November 9   4:00 p.m.
"Minimalism and the '60's"

all free and open to the public

art films
art films
art films
art films
art films

Sponsored by the Public and Cultural Affairs Committee of The College of Staten Island   / CUNY

Betti Broadwater Haft: "Letterforms Are Sacred to Me"

Anne Galperin

Author's note: *I came to know Betti Haft through the* Photo-Lettering's One Line Manual of Styles, *which appeared in the trove of books and supplies my father-in-law gifted me upon retiring from his career as an ad agency art director.*

The manual is a mind-boggling compendium: 470 pages, 18 samples per page. I'd looked through it often, but during 2018's summer break, the list of 252 designers showcased in the volume made me stop short. Sprinkled in with the likes of Milton Glaser and Bradbury Thompson were the names of just 12 women.

I decided to try and find them. Several had died before I began my search. One I couldn't locate. I wrote two with an invitation to talk. Betti called me back. Since then, we've had several rich conversations about her typeface, life, and design. Betti is witty, precise, and eloquent, an elegant amalgam of the European and southern and northeastern US influences that shaped her.

Betti Haft, *Art Films*, College of Staten Island, ca. 1977, poster. Progressive slicing off of the repeated text evokes the motion of a filmstrip. It appears that Haft custom rendered her own typeface to improve the relationship between the lowercase *f*'s ascender and the *i*'s tittle.

Betti Haft, née Broadwater, was born on January 4, 1933, at her paternal grandmother's home in Lookout Mountain, Tennessee. She began her schooling at her granny's knee, reading with her from the King James Bible, the *Chattanooga Times*'s funny pages, and *Grimms' Fairy Tales*. Thus began Haft's love of letterforms and text, ideas and meaning.

In 1941, Haft and her parents relocated to New York to live with her maternal grandparents in Upper Manhattan. "When I got to New York, my new classmates had already learned how to write cursive, but I had not," Haft says. "So I had to pick it up from my friend who was a lefty. I imitated her backward slant—very jazzy!"[1] Even as a child, Haft dove into the culture of the city, spending hours at the Metropolitan Museum of Art and the American Museum of Natural History.

Haft attended Washington Irving High School, where she was one of five thousand girls of diverse backgrounds and nationalities thronging the eleven-story building at 40 Irving Place. A high-achieving student, she was on the vocational—rather than the academic—track and already working odd jobs to help out at home.

As a high school senior during McCarthyism Haft was affected by the Feinberg Law, a New York State law—repealed in 1967—that removed individuals identified as subversive or communist from public schools. One of her history teachers was fired under the law, resulting in Haft's Regents exam score being downgraded, which disqualified her from receiving a college scholarship. Fortunately, the Workshop School of Advertising Art offered one-year scholarships, and Haft was an awardee.

The Workshop School was Haft's initiation into design. When she began taking classes there during fall 1949, the school was flooded with World War II vets returning to school on the G.I. Bill. "I was one of three girls in a sea of men," Haft says. "I learned a lot from those guys: they were not there to play. We went to school at night because we couldn't afford to go during the day. We were there to work with a degree of seriousness."

Haft's early handwriting challenges were ultimately redressed in a calligraphy class taught by Paul Standard. "Standard asked the students why we were taking the class, and I said because I had to," Haft says. "He said, 'That's all right, dear, you'll learn.' And by the time the course concluded, I had."

Creating and working with letterforms became Haft's passion. Standard was a staunch mentor, "nagging" her until she took two tests to apply to the Cooper Union's free night-school certificate program. "It was my last hope," Haft says. "I couldn't afford anything and had to work during the day."

Haft passed both exams and secured a spot. During her three years at Cooper, she became highly proficient at specifying type and laying out precise comps in the school's printshop. The Haber ruler had just been introduced, and its point, pica, and inch markings made manual type calculations easier. "I learned to be useful on the scene and could do everything, design to production," Haft says. "No other woman was doing this. If you could set type accurately and quickly, it was a really well-paying job."

As Haft saw upon entering the workforce, prospects for women designers were largely limited to a ghetto of gendered venues including apparel design studios and homemaking and fashion magazines. There were few opportunities in design and ad agencies and a dearth of genuine interest in supporting emergent female designers.

Haft's professionalism was not always well met. At one job interview, she recalls, "I had a big portfolio with handles, and I had to use it as a shield," describing the predatory advances of her interviewer. "[I undid] the office door lock behind my back to get out of the art director's office. I got out of there as fast as I could." Still, she got the job offer. But it included "Thursdays with the boss." She declined. As she saw it, there were two options: "Either be treated as a bimbo or an alien."

Through connections from the Cooper Union, Haft landed a job working at the now-defunct pharmaceutical advertising firm William Douglas McAdams, which from the late 1940s on was owned by Dr. Arthur Sackler, who became well known for the fortune he made promoting, and later producing, pharmaceuticals. Haft was an assistant art director of *Spectrum*, a Pfizer pharmaceutical eight-pager directed at doctors and inserted into issues of the *Journal of the American Medical Association*. It was a sought-after position, but Haft found the McAdams office culture to be often testosterone-driven and sexist.

Haft soon left McAdams and signed up with an employment agency, which placed her at the offices of the Girl Scouts of America. While she'd been pounding the pavement, Haft had also contacted Will Burtin's studio, hoping to get an interview with the renowned German émigré designer. Three months later, the studio called. Haft recalls,

> I didn't even think I would get in the door, but I was welcomed. Will was interested in the fact that I had studied with Paul

Standard and that I was really interested in typefaces and had done a number of typographic covers for *Spectrum*. He did the usual thing and said, "When we have a vacancy I'll call you." I felt very grateful he didn't kick me out of the office. I wasn't one of the people who had poured out of Yale. I was just delighted he would see me.

Haft wound up working at Will Burtin Incorporated from 1955 to 1958. It was the post–World War II moment of accelerated economic growth, and Haft worked in an advertising industry high on federal tax breaks, in which war-dividend technological developments converged with émigré artists, designers, and photographers for whom modernism was a progressive ethos.

It was a fortuitous career break. "Will really changed my life," Haft says. "He was one of the most ethical people I've ever met, everything you'd wish for. He treated me with the utmost respect and gave me opportunities. It was an enormous gift."

Haft was one of several young creatives in this rich milieu. George Klauber, a former student of Burtin at Pratt Institute, was a studio manager. His boyfriend, Andy Warhol, was often commissioned to do illustrations. The photographer Roman Vishniac, best known for his documentation of Eastern European Jewish shtetl life before the Holocaust, often freelanced with the studio. Among other accomplishments was Vishniac's pioneering method of photomicroscopy, showcased in images for *Scope*, a magazine for the Upjohn pharmaceutical company and a major Burtin studio account. Hilde Burtin, Will Burtin's wife at the time, contributed valuable research to studio projects. Other, mostly European designers, among them Burton Kramer and Yves Zimmermann, joined the staff for nine-month periods on guest visas.

Burtin's stellar reputation and close relationship with prestige clients helped leverage a constant stream of groundbreaking projects. A highly skilled information designer, particularly of scientific phenomena, Burtin pitched to and received funding from Upjohn to create a large-scale scientific model, twenty-four feet wide and twelve feet tall, of a red blood cell. Haft was among the studio designers creating maquettes for the cell model, which was exhibited to much acclaim at a 1958 American Medical Association meeting in San Francisco.

The United States Information Agency (USIA) was another major Burtin account. Haft was assigned to a USIA project highlighting the growth of an American town: Kalamazoo, Michigan

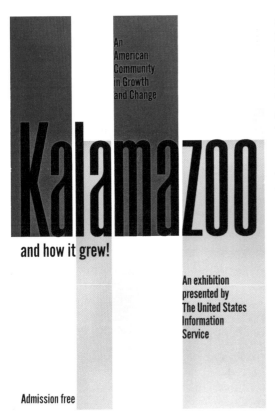

An
American
Community
in Growth
and Change

Kalamazoo

and how it grew!

An exhibition
presented by
The United States
Information
Service

Admission free

Will Burtin Studio, *Kalamazoo and How It Grew*, **ca. 1958, poster. This rendering of "Kalamazoo" is an early incarnation of the typeface that Haft would ultimately refine for Photo-Lettering Inc.**

(not coincidentally where Upjohn was headquartered). It began with a poster. "I had an hour and half to do it," Haft says. "Yves Zimmermann looked at it and [verbally] tore the lettering apart: it was 'terrible.'" Zimmerman had been trained to letter with a brush, while Haft was taught to use ruling pens. "We had a big discussion about it, and I said, 'OK, you know so much, why don't you teach me?'"

Zimmerman began mentoring her. "We would stay behind whenever we had an hour or so," she says. "He would give me instructions, and we would design an alphabet.... In the middle of this, he had to leave because his time [in the studio] was up, and he said, 'Well, I guess you'll have to go to Switzerland and study with my teachers.'"

Haft's path to Switzerland was not that simple: while designing an article to appear in *Scope*, she met Georgine Oeri, the feature's author. The women became fast friends, and Oeri became another mentor to Haft. An art critic and educator, Oeri was a staff manager and lecturer at the Guggenheim Museum, an instructor at Parsons School of Design, and, coincidentally, the art consultant for the Switzerland-based Geigy Chemical Corporation. She suggested Haft pursue a position at Geigy, as they were about to move their corporate design account in-house to their American headquarters in Ardsley, New York.

EUROPEAN GROTESQUES designed in weights to meet
EUROPEAN GROTESQUES designed in weights to meet
EUROPEAN GROTESQUES designed in weights to meet
EUROPEAN GROTESQUES designed in weights to meet

CONTEMPORARY DESIGN with impact offers visual
CONTEMPORARY DESIGN with impact offers visual
CONTEMPORARY DESIGN with impact offers visual
CONTEMPORARY DESIGN with impact offers visual

VISUAL EXCITEMENT follows alternate patterns
VISUAL EXCITEMENT follows alternate patterns
VISUAL EXCITEMENT follows alternate patterns
VISUAL EXCITEMENT follows alternate patterns

PORTÉE PAR LA VAGUE de la haute conjoncture Hollens
PORTÉE PAR LA VAGUE de la haute conjoncture Hollens
PORTÉE PAR LA VAGUE de la haute conjoncture Hollens
PORTÉE PAR LA VAGUE de la haute conjoncture Hollens   965

Photo-Lettering 1964 Alphabet Supplement cover and page 965, featuring type specimens of Broadwater-Haft Grotesque Narrow 4, Broadwater-Haft Grotesque Narrow 7, and Broadwater-Haft Grotesque Narrow 9. Haft Grotesque maintains its original x-height and overall proportions, but the weights Haft drew for PLINC feature increased visual tension and a more emphatic, squared-off contour.

Haft's experience and relationships with people working in all facets of the design industry made her a perfect candidate to direct Geigy's in-house production. She became the first American to work in the studio.

It was a demanding job: Haft lived in Queens, worked in Westchester, drove to Manhattan after hours to deliver type specs to the phototypesetter, and waited for hours to pick up the galleys for paste-up. Then she drove back home to Queens to sleep and back to Westchester for the next day's work. What kept Haft going—besides her work ethic and trusty VW Beetle—was the contract she had arranged with Geigy: she would be sent to the company's Basel design atelier for one year to take a half-time position while attending the Schule für Gestaltung Basel, the highly influential Basel School of Design.

Haft transferred to Switzerland in April 1959, setting type and taking design classes with the likes of Armin Hoffmann and Emil Ruder. She recalls Ruder's teaching style as exceptionally student centered: "Ruder was a lovely person; his criticisms were constructive. He was very generous in showing me things. He really gave me a lot of time. It was a remarkable experience, doubly so because women didn't [typically attend the School of Design]." Haft made friends with the few women at work and in class, among them the American designer Barbara Stauffacher Solomon, who also worked in the Geigy atelier.

A few months before Haft left for Switzerland, she'd begun dating Leon Haft, a Bronx-born architect. Though Haft assumed that the relationship would end once she left New York, Leon kept in touch and soon proposed. After a whirlwind wedding week in Peekskill, New York, Haft brought Leon back to Switzerland for the remainder of the year. To her amusement, Haft went from being the suspect "Fraulein Broadwater," an unmarried and outspoken American, to being "Frau Haft," the highly respected architect's wife. Leon went to work for Geigy as well. When the year ended, the couple honeymooned throughout Europe before returning home.

Back in New York, both Haft and her husband were freelancing, and she often collaborated with him and his clients. Needing type, she got back in touch with Aaron Burns, a friend and the director of design and type at the typesetting house Composing Room, with whom she'd been working since her Burtin studio days. Betti and Leon contemplated their next move: Join the Peace Corps? Apply for a Fulbright? Start a family?

They decided to have a child. Haft felt the impetus to revive and complete the typeface project she had begun under Yves Zimmerman's informal tutelage back in her Burtin studio days. Aaron Burns put Haft in touch with Photo-Lettering, Inc. (PLINC) to vet the work, and they commissioned the project.

> I was working on the alphabet when I went into labor....I had to get as much done as I could. [Leon and I] shared a big table in our studio, and when the pains got to be acute, I called the obstetrician and said, "I think it's going to be now." And she said, "Hold on, wait until midnight to check into the hospital. Because they'll charge you for an extra day just for those few minutes." So I continued working.

The Hafts' daughter, Nina, arrived in summer 1963—about the same time as Haft Grotesque 7, a condensed and curvaceous midweight, sans serif, made-for-film typeface with calligraphic roots.

The Haft family was preparing to make a move to Cambridge, Massachusetts, so that Leon could accept a position at The Architects Collaborative (TAC), a prestigious American firm for which Walter Gropius was senior founding member. Betti enjoyed being part of a community of young mothers there: "We formed a sort of unit. It was a time of really good will—everyone was helping each other."

This was a busy and rewarding time for Haft. PLINC requested two more weights of Haft Grotesque, which again had to be hand-rendered. "I had already figured out how the type was going to be, but I had to figure out the *xyz* and draw them," she says. "I did that at night, and it took about two years."

The Haft Grotesque family embodied Haft's conviction, based on her experience and training, that calligraphy and typography had, as she says, "something to do with each other. I did a grotesque that was based on calligraphic thicks and thins. That was its feature. They were teaching that calligraphy was a separate thing. I wanted to bring the two together."

Betti and Leon's second child, Jamie, arrived in 1966. Haft finished the Haft Grotesque family, worked on projects for Harvard University, and freelanced for TAC.

In 1968, Leon accepted a position in New York, and he and Haft moved the family to Queens. Over the next several years, Haft took up illustration, production, and design for various employers and worked in house at the American Museum of Natural History, developing materials for the hall of minerals as it was designed, built, and opened to the public.

Haft remained friendly with colleagues from her Burtin days, among them Bob Hagenhofer, one of the studio managers. When Hagenhofer left a post in the reprographics department at Staten Island Community College (now the College of Staten Island, CSI), he suggested that Haft interview for his job. Leon was facing health challenges, so it made sense for Haft to be the primary breadwinner. She held the position—with its two-and-a-half-hour round-trip commute—for more than twenty years. Haft managed a staff of ten and designed and ran the in-house production of thousands of printed artifacts for every facet of CSI's operations.

Haft continued her formal education while working at CSI. In 1979, based on her portfolio, the Cooper Union upgraded her certificate degree to a BA. She subsequently earned a master of liberal arts from CSI.

Ephemera for the College of Staten Island, ca. 1977–97. Haft's two decades of work for the College of Staten Island demonstrates her wit, visual panache, and principled belief in design as a vehicle for effective—and often delightful—communication.

Despite the typical economic constraints on design at public educational institutions, Haft's work for CSI stands out for its clarity, joyous use of color, and typographic verve. Haft used her own typeface and custom-designed headline type for routine projects. Her work reflected her ethos that no project was too small or insignificant to deliver both information and delight to the user.

Haft's career—or, in her words, the way she "made a living"—spanned fifty years. Looking back on her experiences, Haft notes,

> It's not because I was so wonderful [a talent] but because I was in the right place at the right time and was able to take advantage of that. Many people were not so lucky. The women who made it had to go through so much. You wonder how they did it. The implications were that they were sleeping with the right people. I get so incensed, because I knew many women along the line for whom things didn't go so well. So I think there's something to be said about the women who managed to survive, take care of themselves, and have integrity.

With characteristic self-deprecation, Betti Haft summed up her career: "I'm not one of the stars, but I did do a little something along the way." Yes, she did.

David Montross
TROIKA

Afterword
Martha Scotford

While they may have felt potent and gender appropriate at one time, I am tired of the too-common metaphors used for women's endeavors coming from handwork: weaving, knitting, fabric, threads, yarn, skeins, and quilts, among others. These seem overly material, confining, and quaint. Natural science can provide better: I prefer to employ the metaphor of tree branches and roots. We can go further: connected to trees' roots are fungal tendrils creating a supporting mat of watering and nurturing mycelium underlying everything, resembling the structures that have long permitted women to support one another.

In this collection of essays I have sensed an expanding set of connections among scholars (mostly but not all women) who are working to uncover significant efforts by women in fields of visual and verbal communication. A growing mat that is sending up fungi/flags to mark interesting, instructive, and often unknown examples.

When I read nonfiction, I go to the bibliography and acknowledgments first. I want to know where authors have been and with whom

Ellen Raskin, cover of *Troika*, David Montross, 1963. Raskin embraces modernist abstraction in her illustration and lettering.

they have connected. I note, different from when I was first involved in research, an increasing use of internet resources; this suggests an enlarging and accessible body of material about women's work, organized by individuals and institutions.

Though digital archives are to be celebrated, I have found a different sense of discovery, and even joy, when using more traditional material archives. If I may digress, I still remember feeling thrilled (and also a bit overwhelmed) as I started the case study project based on my essay "Neat and Messy History" and found that designer Cipe Pineles's archives at Rochester Institute of Technology comprised seventy bankers boxes. These were relatively new to RIT and had not been "processed." For me, even better. Yes, I had to construct my own finding guide, but the materials appeared to be directly from her filing cabinets and drawers. Because no curator had viewed, evaluated, and organized them, I could see her organization. I could see the records and files but also the connected personal ephemera (which might not have survived curation). My research started with Pineles and what she told me through her boxes. Then I moved on to family and friends. I didn't know the mantra at the time, but the biographer Robert Caro (of Robert Moses and LBJ fame) says in his memoir, *Working*, "Turn every page." This is good advice.

I know some of these authors only by reputation and was previously aware of just two of the subjects. The essays present a wide cultural and political context for design activities. Graphic design is a capacious umbrella, and the topics show this: from the hand (craft, not a bad word) of type drawing and typesetting to printing, from illustration and design to larger-scale production and publication, and ultimately to audience consumption and reception. Everyone is a worker, and there are many collaborators, with varying life and working conditions. There is no sense of hierarchy in the materials, products, and people of this history; high form and star individuals are not important.

There are some themes: the common struggle for women's work/life balance, the presence of women in the backrooms of production who sometimes refuse to stay there—women ready to seize opportunity and women who discover talents as they learn new skills. I find a welcome reminder of the importance of print magazines as vehicles of culture and politics, and as historical documents.

The writing styles vary, from a formal academic writing to a more demotic language, perhaps imagining different audiences. Some of the essays relate a personal connection with the subject or her work, beyond a scholarly interest; only one has been able to interview her subject. Subject matter and authors present an important geographical expansion. Too often, even though we use the same language, English and American projects do not cross the ocean. This volume includes work from other continents and languages.

This is all very encouraging.

It is most gratifying to have read these essays and to apprehend the range and differences gathered here—toward the common goal of deepening our knowledge of women in creative history. Teaching has many rewards: short-term satisfactions in the classroom and the longer-term gratification of watching former students come into their professional lives. Research and writing take time; there is a long feedback loop before one can see if one has made a difference. I appreciate those rewards in these writers' extension of ideas and practices I proposed years ago. Carry on!

February 2021

Acknowledgments

First and foremost, I would like to thank the authors featured in *Baseline Shift*. Their critical research, as well as the care they put into their essays and our correspondence as we worked collaboratively to put the materials together for this book, are the *only* reason it now exists.

Baseline Shift would also not have been possible without the original project it stemmed from, which I worked on with Kate Bingaman-Burt. Even though our projects went separate ways, she has been a rock for me.

I would also like to thank the lively and incredibly smart and inspiring group of design historians, educators, and curators I meet with regularly to discuss curriculum, research, and the general revolution that is occurring in our field right now. I'm lucky to have so many people to talk to and learn from, who span years, backgrounds, and interests within graphic design history as a discipline.

For the book itself, I'm grateful to my first-ever book editor, Sara Stemen, for guiding me through this somewhat complicated process, and to my friend and mentor, Louise Sandhaus, for her sage publishing guidance. I'm thankful to Andi Zeisler, who helped this designer mold her words beyond the simply serviceable. I'm grateful to the librarians who helped me access the archival materials of Ellen Raskin before—but more importantly, during—a global pandemic. And thanks to indexer Summer Nishan of Twin Oaks Community, for her care in creating the index.

I'm always aware of those who led the way in terms of design and design history. While there are too many to list in full, I would like to acknowledge the writings and ideas of Martha Scotford, Ellen Lupton, Louise Sandhaus, Lorraine Wild, Johanna Drucker, Emily McVarish, and Steven Heller, who have been important for the progression of our history and for my own evolution as an educator and historian.

Finally, of course, I would like to thank my family, blood and chosen—Sean, Anya, Angela, and my dad for listening to my very frequent talk about women in graphic design history—now, in the past, and forever.

Notes

Introduction

1 Martha Scotford, "Messy History vs. Neat History: Toward an Expanded View of Women in Graphic Design," *Visible Language* 28, no. 4 (Fall 1994): 367.

2 Scotford, "Messy History," 367.

3 Scotford, "Messy History," 369.

4 Cheryl D. Holmes-Miller, "Black Designers: Forward in Action (Part IV)," *Print*, October 15, 2020, https://www.printmag.com/post/black-designers-forward-in-action-part-iv.

"Her Greatest Work Lay in Decorative Design": Angel De Cora, Ho-Chunk Artist, ca. 1869–1919

1 Angel's surname was passed down from Jean Descaris, a seventeenth-century immigrant to New France, whose son married a Ho-Chunk woman. Over the centuries, this name has been rendered a multitude of ways, including "Decary." The Ho-Chunk commonly use "Decorah" or "Decora," but Angel signed her paintings "de Cora," to highlight her name's French origins. "DeCora" is how most people rendered her name during her lifetime, and this form is still used by some family members today. I use "De Cora" in this text, except when quoting a different spelling. Elaine Goodale Eastman, "In Memoriam: Angel De Cora Dietz," *American Indian* (Spring 1919), 51–52.

2 Julia DeCora Lukecart to Thomas Hughes, 29 October 1920, Thomas Hughes Papers, Minnesota Historical Society, St. Paul. For more on De Cora's life and career, see Linda M. Waggoner, *Fire Light: The Life of Angel De Cora, Winnebago Artist* (Norman, OK: University of Oklahoma Press, 2008).

3 Tom Hill Sr. and Richard Hill, eds., *Creation's Journey: Native American Identity and Belief* (New York: National Museum of the American Indian, 1994).

4 John C. Ewers, Helen M. Mangelsdorf, and William S. Wierbowski, *Images of a Vanished Life: Plains Indian Drawings from the Collection of the Pennsylvania Academy of the Fine Arts* (1956; repr., Philadelphia: Pennsylvania Academy of the Fine Arts, 1985), 10.

5 Patricia Trenton, ed., *Independent Spirits: Women Painters of the American West, 1890–1945* (Berkeley: Autry Museum of Western Heritage in association with University of California Press, 1995), 264–65.

6 Reprinted in *Southern Workman*, August 1894, Angel DeCora file, Hampton University Archives, Hampton, Virginia.

7 *Southern Workman*, July 1896, Angel DeCora file, Hampton University Archives, Hampton, Virginia.

8 Cora W. Folsom, "The Careers of Three Indian Women," *Congregationalist and Christian World*, March 12, 1904, Angel DeCora file, Hampton University Archives, Hampton, Virginia.

9 Folsom, "Careers of Three Indian Women."

10 "Catlin's Successor in Indian Portrait Painting," reprinted in *Southern Workman*, September 11, 1897, Angel DeCora file, Hampton University Archives, Hampton, Virginia.

11 "Pencil and Palette," *Philadelphia Inquirer*, February 13, 1898, Angel DeCora file, Hampton University Archives, Hampton Virginia.

12 "F. Schoonover interview, 1966," Box 2B, Howard Pyle Manuscript Collection, Helen Farr Sloan Library and Archives, Delaware Art Museum, Wilmington, DE.

13 Anna Hoopes, "Memories of Howard Pyle," 1935, Box 2A, Howard Pyle Manuscript Collection, Helen Farr Sloan Library and Archives, Delaware Art Museum, Wilmington, DE.

14 Natalie Curtis, "An American Indian Artist," *Outlook Magazine* (January 14, 1920), 64–66.

15 Howard Pyle to Cora Folsom, n.d., Angel DeCora file, Hampton University Archives, Hampton, Virginia.

16 Angel DeCora-Dietz, "Angel DeCora—An Autobiography," *The Red Man by Red Men* 3 (March 1911): 279–80, 285.

17 Curtis, "An American Indian Artist."

18 Curtis, "An American Indian Artist."

19 Although the chapter is titled "Dakota," the pictograph was drawn by the Lakota chief Short Bull (featured prominently in Ewers's work). Curtis used an umbrella term common in her day to encompass the Siouxian peoples, Lakota, Nakota, and Dakota.

20 Curtis, "An American Indian Artist."

21 *The Arrow* 3, no. 49 (August 23, 1907), Cumberland County Historical Society, Carlisle Pennsylvania.

22 *The Arrow* 3, no. 49.

23 Angel DeCora-Dietz, "Native Indian Art," *Report of the Executive on the Proceedings of the First Annual Conference of the Society of American Indians Held at the University of Ohio, Columbus, Ohio, October 12–17, 1911* (Washington, DC: Society of American Indians, 1912), 87.

24 Dietz was actually a German American posing as a Sioux. See Linda M. Waggoner, "On Trial: The Washington R*dskins Wily Mascot: Coach William 'Lone Star' Dietz," *Montana: The Magazine of Western History* (Spring 2013), 24–47.

25 A Congressional investigation into Carlisle's sports program revealed the Indian Art Department was no longer adequately funded by the federal government. De Cora quit teaching in 1916 and took on other work as an artist. Carlisle Indian School closed in 1918, partly due to the growing unpopularity of off-reservation boarding schools as well as the advent of World War I, but mostly because the US military reclaimed the land it had leased to the school for a military hospital.

26 Curtis, "An American Indian Artist."

A Black Renaissance Woman: Louise E. Jefferson

1 Edie Lynch, "Louise E. Jefferson," Amistad Research Center.

2 Lynch, "Louise E. Jefferson."

3 Louise E. Jefferson, "Everything Dovetails: Louise E. Jefferson," interview by T. J. Banks, *Sketch People*, March 1984.

4 Lester B. Granger, "The Credit Line is Lou's," *Opportunity* 25 (Spring 1947): 91–92.

5 Jefferson, "Everything Dovetails."

6 Lynch, "Louise E. Jefferson."

7 Lynch, "Louise E. Jefferson."

8 "Harlem Artists Guild," *Wikipedia*, Wikimedia Foundation, last edited February 10, 2018, https://en.wikipedia.org/wiki/Harlem_Artists_Guild.

9 Lynch, Edie, "Louise E. Jefferson."

10 Granger, "Credit Line."

11 "A Remarkable Inclusive Map by Louise E. Jefferson Highlighting Dislocation in the United States During WWII," *Boston Rare Maps*, https://bostonraremaps.com/inventory/louise-e-jefferson-uprooted-people-1945/.

12 Granger, "Credit Line."

13 Jana King, "Louise E. Jefferson," Design Journeys, AIGA, updated 2012, https://www.aiga.org/design-journeys-louise-e-jefferson.

14 Lynch, "Louise E. Jefferson."

15 Lynch, "Louise E. Jefferson."

16 Granger, " Credit Line."

Women of the Federal Art Project Poster Division

1 William E. Leuchtenburg, "Franklin D. Roosevelt: The American Franchise," U.S. Presidents, The Presidency, UVA/Miller Center, accessed September 10, 2020, https://millercenter.org/president/fdroosevelt/the-american-franchise.

2 Barbara Melosh, *Engendering Culture: Manhood and Womanhood in New Deal Public Art and Theater* (Washington, DC: Smithsonian Institution Press, 1991), 1.

3 Francis Valentine O'Connor, *Federal Support for the Visual Arts: The New Deal and Now* (Greenwich, CT: New York Graphic Society, 1969), 192.

4 O'Connor, *Federal Support*, 29.

5 William Francis McDonald, *Federal Relief Administration and the Arts: The Origins and Administrative History of the Arts Projects of the Works Progress Administration* (Columbus, OH: Ohio State University Press, 1968), 433.

6 Linda Flint McClelland, *Building the National Parks: Historic Landscape and Construction* (Baltimore: John Hopkins University Press: 1997), 425.

7 McClelland, *Building the National Parks*, 428.

8 Susan Merritt, "Celebrate 100 Years of the National Park Service with a Hunt for Lost Posters," *AIGA Eye on Design*, August 4, 2015, https://eyeondesign.aiga.org/celebrate-100-years-of-the-national-parks-service-with-a-hunt-for-lost-posters/. Merritt's article describes little of Waugh's career or contributions beyond the posters' design.

9 Robert L. Leslie, "Dorothy Waugh: A Discussion of Her Work," *A-D* (December/January 1941–42), 43.

10 Leslie, "Dorothy Waugh," 43.

11 *New York School of Fine and Applied Art Course Catalog 1941–1942* (New York: New York School of Fine and Applied Art, 1941), 8; *Parsons School of Design Course Catalog 1942–1943* (New York: New York School of Fine and Applied Art, 1942), 6.

12 Leslie, "Dorothy Waugh," 44.

13 Benjamin F. Shearer, *Home Front Heroes: A Biographical Dictionary of Americans during Wartime*, vol. 1 (Westport, CT: Greenwood Press, 2007), 21.

14 Shearer, *Home Front Heroes*, 21.

15 Kristan H. McKinsey, "The Perseverance of Mildred Waltrip," *Illinois Heritage: A Publication of the Illinois Historical Society* (March/April 2020), 14.

16 McKinsey, "Perseverance of Mildred Waltrip," 16.

17 Judy Pasternak, "Murals' Racial Images Confront Worldly Suburb: Stereotypes Featured in School's WPA Artworks Disturb Some Oak Park Parents. Specter of Censorship Upsets Others," *Los Angeles Times*, March 2, 1995, https://www.latimes.com/archives/la-xpm-1995-03-02-mn-37871-story.html.

18 Elaine Templin, "Enjoying Festivals with Katherine Milhous," *Elementary English* 34, no. 7 (November 1957): 436.

19 Miranda Orso, "Katherine Milhous," Pennsylvania Center for the Book, Pennsylvania State University, updated 2018, https://pabook.libraries.psu.edu/literary-cultural-heritage-map-pa/bios/Milhous__Katherine.

20 Templin, "Enjoying Festivals," 437.

21 Templin, "Enjoying Festivals," 439.

One for the Books: Ellen Raskin's Design, Lettering, and Illustration

1 Lynne Yun, "History of the Alphabet: Part 1," April 16, 2020, YouTube video, 27:22, https://youtu.be/acYR3Hpk-Oo.

2 Martha Scotford, "Messy History vs. Neat History: Toward an Expanded View of Women in Graphic Design," *Visible Language* 28, no. 4 (Fall 1994): 381–82.

3 Ellen Raskin, interview with Center for Television Production, University of Wisconsin Green Bay, August 23, 1983, transcript, Cooperative Children's Book Center, University of Wisconsin, Madison.

4 Raskin, interview.

5 Raskin, interview.

6 Marilynn Strasser Olson, *Ellen Raskin* (Boston: Twayne Publishers, 1991), 3.

7 Alice Bach, "Ellen Raskin: Some Clues about Her Life," *Horn Book Magazine* 61, no. 2 (1985): 162–67.

8 James W. Roginski, *Behind the Covers: Interviews with Authors and Illustrators of Books for Children and Young Adults* (Littleton, CO: Libraries Unlimited, 1985), 167.

9 "Ellen Raskin," in *UXL Junior DISCovering Authors* (Detroit, MI: UXL, 2003), Gale In Context: High School, accessed January 6, 2021, https://link.gale.com/apps/doc/EJ2110100348/GPS?u=oregon_sl&sid=GPS&xid=4f65add9.

10 Raskin, interview.

11 Raskin, interview

12 Arlie Hochschild with Anne Machung, *The Second Shift: Working Parents and the Revolution at Home* (New York: Viking, 1989).

13 Raskin, interview.

14 Roginski, *Behind the Covers*, 171.

16 Aggie Toppins, "Can We Teach Graphic Design History Without the Cult of Hero Worship?," *AIGA Eye on Design*, May 29, 2020, accessed October, 15 2020, https://eyeondesign.aiga.org/can-we-teach-graphic-design-history-without-the-cult-of-hero-worship/.

Bea Feitler: The *Sir* to *Ms.* Years

1 Feitler said, "It should flow. It should have its ups and downs. It should have a beginning and an end. It should not be designed as a spread-by-spread concept. The closest thing to motion is editorial design." Robert A. Propper, "Bea Feitler Sense Ability," *Graphics Today* (July–August 1977), 23–32.

2 A comprehensive book about her work was published in Brazil only in 2012 by her nephew and the Brazilian graphic designer André Stolarski. André Stolarski and Bruno Feitler, *O Design de Bea Feitler* (São Paulo: Cosac Naify, 2012), 9–10.

3 In a 1978 interview for the Brazilian edition of *Interview* magazine, Feitler shares some impressions of life as a freelancer: "If you have a psychological structure that allows you to be calm and not wake up in the middle of the night without knowing how it will be in the morning, if you are going to have work or not, life as a freelancer is great. This idea that people have of the freelance professional is that of a person who works two days and spends the rest of the week looking at the sea (in the case of Rio de Janeiro) or at the cinema (in New York). This idea is totally false because you work harder. Maybe not with regular hours, but social life becomes a lot due to work." Vania Toledo and Bea Feitler, *Interview* (February 1978), 18–19.

4 Ruy Castro and Maria Amélia Melo, *O melhor da Revista Sr.* (São Paulo: Imprensa Oficial do Estado, 2012).

5 Chico Homem de Melo, "A revista Senhor está para a ilustração assim como Realidade está para a fotografia," *Design Gráfico Brasileiro: Anos 60* (São Paulo: Cosac Naify, 2006), 90–173.

6 Carlos Leonam, "Retrato de Bea," *Jornal do Brasil*, month and day, 1962, 36–37.

7 José Emílio Rondeau, "Bea Feitler—A carioca que dignificou as artes gráficas no Brasil e no mundo," *Jornal O Globo*, April 13, 1982, 37.

8 Chico Homem de Melo, "Design de livros: muitas capas, muitas caras," *Design Gráfico Brasileiro: Anos 60* (São Paulo: Cosac Naify, 2006), 54–91.

9 As mentioned by Jaguar in Feitler's obituary, published in Rondeau, "Bea Feitler—A carioca."

10 Leonam, "Retrato de Bea," 36–37.

11 Philip B. Meggs, "Bea Feitler," AIGA, September 1, 1989, https://www.aiga.org /medalist-beafeitler.

12 Caderno Mais #19 [undated], Bea Feitler Papers, KA.0014.01, box 5, folder 4, New School Archives and Special Collections, New School, New York.

13 "Her Story: 1971—Present," *Ms.*, accessed September 4, 2020, https://msmagazine.com /about/. Amy Erdman Farrell, *Yours in Sisterhood: Ms. Magazine and the Promise of Popular Feminism* (Chapel Hill: University of North Carolina Press, 1998).

14 Propper, "Bea Feitler Sense Ability," 30.

15 Suzana Sichel, "Esta senhora não participa do movimento feminista americano. Mas trabalha (muito) para ele," *Resenha Judaica*, March 1973.

16 Hildegard Angel, "Bea Feitler, ou como vencer nos States fazendo muita força," *Jornal do Brasil/ Revista JN*, January 17, 1975, 3.

17 Andre Leon Talley, "Judging a Book by Its Cover," *Women's Wear Daily*, October 8, 1976.

18 Jornal do Brasil, "Bea Feitler—uma ipanemense na história das artes gráficas," *Caderno B*, April 18, 1982, 9.

19 Propper, "Bea Feitler Sense Ability," 26.

20 Talley, "Judging a Book."

▟

By Women, for Women:
Suffragist Graphic Design

1 Both gains and losses occurred in the suffrage movement. For instance, women in New Jersey in the eighteenth century had the right to vote, but that was taken away from them in 1807; Utah granted women suffrage in 1870, only to have Congress invalidate its action in the 1880s.

2 Though the amendment was written to cover all American women, it did not encompass, for instance, Indigenous or Japanese American women, who were at the time of its passing not considered citizens and thus excluded.

3 Robert P. J. Cooney Jr., "A Brief Summary of the 1911 Campaign," California Women Suffrage Centennial, California Secretary of State, accessed June 29, 2020, https://www.sos.ca.gov /elections/celebrating-womens-suffrage /california-women-suffrage-centennial/.

4 Allison Lange, *Picturing Political Power: Images in the Women's Suffrage Movement* (Chicago: University of Chicago Press, 2020), 180.

5 Connie Koenenn, "Female Designers Finally Get Their Due in an Exhibition at New York's Bard Graduate Center for Studies in the Decorative Arts," *Los Angeles Times*, November 9, 2000, https://www.latimes.com/archives/la-xpm -2000-nov-09-cl-49097-story.html.

6 "Evelyn Rumsey Cary," Artists, Burchfield Penny Art Center at SUNY Buffalo State, accessed September 2, 2020, https://www .burchfieldpenney.org/artists/artist:evelyn -rumsey-cary/.

7 "Creativity and Persistence: Art that Fueled the Fight for Women's Suffrage," National Endowment for the Arts, August 2020, https:// www.arts.gov/sites/default/files/Creativity-and -Persistence-08.13.20.pdf.

8 Evelyn Rumsey Cary, *Woman's Suffrage…Give Her of the Fruit of Her Hands*, n.d., Schlesinger Library on the History of Women in America, Radcliffe Institute, Harvard University, accessed September 2, 2020, https://images.hollis .harvard.edu/permalink/f/100kie6/HVD _VIAolvwork630196.

9 In the Tumblr of the Virginia Commonwealth University Special Collections and Archives (https://vculibraries.tumblr.com), the back cover of the 1918 edition of *Woman Citizen* is shown with a statement about how suffragists would have easily recognized the quote.

10 Bertha M. Boyé, *Votes for Women*, 1913. Schlesinger Library on the History of Women in America, Radcliffe Institute, Harvard University, accessed July 1, 2020, https://images.hollis .harvard.edu/permalink/f/100kie6/HVD _VIAolvwork391769. Cooney, "Brief Summary."

11 The *Woman's Era*, edited by Josephine St. Pierre Ruffin and Florida Ruffin Ridley (1894– 1897), Atlanta, GA, Emory Women Writers Resource Project, Emory University, http://

womenwriters.digitalscholarship.emory.edu/toc
.php?id=era1.

12 Josephine St. Pierre Ruffin, *Woman's Era* 1,
no. 1 (March 24, 1894), Emory Women Writers
Resource Project, Emory University, 2005,
http://womenwriters.digitalscholarship
.emory.edu/content.php?level=div&id=era1
_01&document=era1.

13 Rodger Streitmatter, *Raising Her Voice:
African-American Women Journalists Who
Changed History* (Lexington: University Press of
Kentucky, 1994), 62.

14 Streitmatter, *Raising Her Voice*, 62.

15 Kaitlin Woods, "'Make the World Better:' The
Woman's Era Club of Boston," Boston National
Historic Park and the Boston African American
National Historic Site, accessed September 7,
2020, https://www.nps.gov/articles/womans
-era-club.htm#_ftn7.

16 Streitmatter, 70.

17 Miranda Orso, "Katherine Milhous,"
Pennsylvania Center for the Book, Pennsylvania
State University, updated 2018, https://pabook
.libraries.psu.edu/literary-cultural-heritage
-map-pa/bios/Milhous__Katherine.

18 Katherine Milhous, "Votes for Women,"
Alcohol, Temperance & Prohibition, Brown Digital
Repository, Brown University Library, https://
repository.library.brown.edu/studio/item
/bdr:29916/.

19 Mary Shepard Greene Blumenschein, *Votes
for Women*, Suffrage Collection, Sophia Smith
Collection of Women's History, Smith College,
accessed August 30, 2020, https://www.smith
.edu/libraries/libs/ssc/popups/popsuffragepc1
.html.

20 "Remarkable Blumenschein Women," *Taos
News*, April 15, 2012, https://www.taosnews
.com/tempo/arts/remarkable-blumenschein
-women/article_b509b315-321f-5492-9a81
-a01a86e3a69f.html.

21 In "Sexual Equality Under the Fourteenth
and Equal Rights Amendments," Ruth Bader
Ginsburg discusses how women's rights were
excluded from the Fourteenth and Fifteenth
Amendments, because they were considered
"not fit subject matter for federal statutory or
constitutional resolution." Ruth Bader Ginsburg,
"Sexual Equality Under the Fourteenth and Equal
Rights Amendments," *Washington University
Law Quarterly* 1 (1979): 161–78, https://
openscholarship.wustl.edu/cgi/viewcontent
.cgi?article=2509&context=law_lawreview.

22 June Hannam, "United States of America," in
International Encyclopedia of Women's Suffrage,
ed. Mitzi Auchterlonie and Katherine Holden
(Santa Barbara, CA: ABC-CLIO, 2000), 300.

23 Hannam, "United States of America," 300.

24 Hannam, "United States of America," 301.

25 Lange, *Picturing Political Power*, 190.

26 Tiffany Lewis argues that the suffrage map
lent legitimacy to the movement. Tiffany Lewis,
"Mapping Social Movements and Leveraging the
U.S. West: The Rhetoric of the Woman Suffrage
Map," *Women's Studies in Communication* 42,
no. 4 (2019): 490–510, https://doi.org/10.1080
/07491409.2019.1676349.

27 Christina E. Dando, "'The Map Proves It:'
Map Use by the American Woman Suffrage
Movement," *Cartographica* 45, no. 4 (Winter
2010): 228, https://doi.org/10.3138/carto
.45.4.221.

28 "The Suffrage Cartoons of Blanche Ames,"
League of Women Voters of Needham, accessed
August 21, 2020, https://lwv-needham.org
/suffrage-cartoons-of-blanche-ames-2/.

29 "The Map Blossoms [Editorial Cartoon
by Blanche Ames Ames," *Woman's Journal
And Suffrage News*, May 22, 1915, Social
Welfare History Project, Special Collections and
Archives, James Branch Cabell Library, Virginia
Commonwealth University Libraries, accessed
September 2, 2020, https://images.socialwelfare
.library.vcu.edu/items/show/130. Other suffrage
maps used the opposite color application. Bertha
Damaris Knobe's 1908 US suffrage map identifies
suffrage states in ink, non-suffrage states in
absence of ink.

30 Laura J. Snyder, "Blanche Ames: Brief Life
of an Intrepid Botanical Illustrator: 1878–1969,"
Harvard Magazine (July–August 2017), https://
harvardmagazine.com/2017/07/blanche-ames.

31 Susan Ware, *Why They Marched: Untold
Stories of the Women Who Fought for the Right to
Vote* (Cambridge, MA: Belknap Press of Harvard
University Press, 2019), 228; "Suffrage Cartoons
of Blanche Ames."

32 John S. Ames, *Borderland: The Life and Times
of Blanche Ames Ames*, directed by Kevin Friend
(Easton, MA: BCN Productions, 2020), film, 55
min., https://www.borderlandthedocumentary.com.

33 Bertha Damaris Knobe, "Votes for Women:
An Object-Lesson," *Harper's Weekly* (April 25,
1908), 20–21, https://digital.library.cornell.edu
/catalog/ss:19343427.

34 Dando, "Map Proves It," 221.

In the Beginning, Woman Was the Sun

1 Mariko Inoue, "Kiyokata's Asasuzu: The Emergence of the Jogakusei Image," *Monumenta Nipponica* 51, no. 4 (November 1996): 440.

2 Nobuhiko Murakami, *Women's Occupations in the Taisho Era* (Tokyo: Domesu, 1983), 127–28.

3 Ronald S. Anderson, *Japan: Three Epochs of Modern Education* (Ann Arbor: University of Michigan Library, 1959), 36–38; "120 Years of Literacy," National Center for Education Statistics, last modified April 17, 2017, https://nces.ed.gov/naal/lit_history.asp.

4 Keiko Tanaka, "Japanese Women's Magazines: The Language of Aspiration," in *The Worlds of Japanese Popular Culture: Gender, Shifting Boundaries and Global Cultures*, ed. D. P. Martinez (Cambridge, U.K.: Cambridge University Press, 1998), 120–22.

5 John R. Clammer, "Consuming Bodies: Constructing and Representing the Female Body in Contemporary Japanese Print Media," in *Women, Media and Consumption in Japan*, ed. Brian Moeran and Lisa Skov (London: Routledge, 2013), 197–219.

6 Ian Lynam, *The Letter I* (Tokyo: Wordshape, 2020), 12–17.

7 Lynam, *The Letter I*, 15.

8 Kon Wajirō and Yoshida Kenkichi, *Modernologio: Kōgengaku* (Tokyo: Shunyōdō, 1930), 86–88.

9 Ian Lynam, "Anything with a Shape Cannot Be Broken," in *Modes of Criticism* 5, ed. Francisco Laranjo (The Hague: Onomatopee, 2019), 50–58.

10 Hiratsuka Raichō, *In the Beginning, Woman Was the Sun: The Autobiography of a Japanese Feminist* (Tokyo: Iwanami Shoten, 1987), 22–28.

11 It is worth noting that Naganuma's cover illustration is a monochrome copy of a painting by the Vienna Secession painter Josef Engelhart.

12 Setsu Shigematsu, *Scream from the Shadows: The Women's Liberation Movement in Japan* (Minneapolis: University of Minnesota Press, 2012), 78–79.

13 Boston Women's Health Book Collective and Judy Norsigian, *Our Bodies, Ourselves: A Book by and for Women*, trans. Akiyama Yōko, Kuwahara Kazuyo, and Yamada Mitsuko (Tokyo: Gōdō Shuppan, 1984).

14 "About Lilmag store," Lilmag, last modified November 12, 2019, http://lilmag.org/?mode=f1.

Collective Authorship and Shared Process: The Madame Binh Graphics Collective

1 Stephen J. Eskilson, *Graphic Design: A New History* (London: Laurence King, 2019), 169; Philip B. Meggs, *A History of Graphic Design* (Hoboken, NJ: John Wiley & Sons, 1998), 455.

2 Mary Patten, *Revolution as an Eternal Dream: The Exemplary Failure of the Madame Binh Graphics Collective* (Chicago: Half Letter Press, 2011), 59.

3 Dan Berger, *The Hidden* 1970s (Piscataway, NJ: Rutgers University Press, 2010), 1–12.

4 See Red Women's Workshop, accessed September 8, 2020, https://seeredwomensworkshop.wordpress.com/; Chicago Women's Liberation Union Herstory Project, accessed September 8, 2020, https://www.cwluherstory.org/our-programs.

5 Madame Binh Graphics Collective, *Silkscreen Class for Women*, flyer, Cooper Union Archive.

6 Tom Wilson, "Paper Walls: Political Posters in an Age of Mass Media," in *West of Center: Art and the Counterculture Experiment in America, 1965–1977*, ed. Elissa Auther and Adam Lerner (Minneapolis: University of Minnesota Press, 2012), 175.

7 Patten, *Revolution as an Eternal Dream*, 15.

8 Patten, *Revolution as an Eternal Dream*, 21.

9 Mary Patten, "We Dissent…Gallery Talk with Mary Patten of Madame Binh Graphics Collective," moderated by Stéphanie Jeanjean, Cooper Union, December 10 2019, audio, 1:22:26, accessed August 6, 2020, http://wedissent.space/talks/.

10 Laura Whitehorn, interview with author, August 13, 2020.

11 Patten, *Revolution as Eternal Dream*, 45.

12 Whitehorn, interview.

13 Patten, *Revolution as Eternal Dream*, 43–45.

14 Patten, *Revolution as Eternal Dream*, 45.

15 Patten, *Revolution as Eternal Dream*, 45–51.

16 Madame Binh Graphics Collective to friend, November 23, 1981, *Madame Binh Graphics Collective Correspondence*, The Freedom Archives, http://freedomarchives.org/Documents/Finder/DOC53_scans/53.MadameBinh.correspondance.pdf.

17 "Anti-Apartheid Solidarity," The Freedom Archives, accessed August 8, 2020, https://search.freedomarchives.org/search.php?view_collection=338&keyword[]=Anti-Springbok+5&no_digital=1.

18 Mary Patten, interview with author, July 20, 2020.

19 *We Dissent…Design of the Women's Movement in New York*, October 2, 2018–December 2, 2018. The Cooper Union, New York, NY.

20 Patten, *Revolution as Eternal Dream*, 45.

21 Gregory Sholette, "Art Out of Joint: Artists' Activism before and after the Cultural Turn," in *The Gulf: High Culture/Hard Labor*, ed. Andrew Ross (New York: OR Books, 2015), 66.

22 Gregory Sholette, "Afterword (Leftists Like Us)," in Mary Patten, *Revolution as an Eternal Dream* (Chicago: Half Letter Press, 2011), 68.

23 Whitehorn, interview.

24 Wilson, "Paper Walls," 164–165.

25 Whitehorn, interview.

26 Patten, Revolution as Eternal Dream, 63.

27 Lucy Lippard, "Foreword: Is Another Art World Possible?," in Gregory Sholette, Delirium and Resistance: *Activist Art and Capitalism* (London: Pluto Press, 2017), xix.

28 "Mission," Women's Center for Creative Work, accessed September 8, 2020, https://corevalues .womenscenterforcreativework.com/.

29 "Prep Work: Working Definitions & Keywords," Toolkit for Cooperative, Collective, and Collaborative Cultural Work, Press Press, accessed August 8, 2020, https://toolkit.press/prep-work .html.

30 "Ground Work: Roles and Hierarchy," Toolkit for Cooperative, Collective, and Collaborative Cultural Work, Press Press, accessed August 8, 2020, https://toolkit.press/ground-work.html.

31 "Mission," Women's Center for Creative Work.

Typist to Typesetter: Norma Kitson and Her Red Lion Setters

1 "Red Lion Setters," Radical & Community Printshops Wiki, http://radicalprintshops.org /doku.php?id=red_lion_setters; Norma Kitson, *Where Sixpence Lives* (London: Hogarth, 1987).

2 Kitson, *Where Sixpence Lives*.

3 Baines, "Red Lion Setters"; Gail Cartmail, interview with author, London, July 23, 2020. Cartmail worked at RLS in the 1980s and is now assistant general secretary of Unite the Union and president of the UK's Trades Union Congress.

4 This study draws on the research of Jess Baines, Gavin Brown, and Helen Yaffe; memories from typesetters and RLS clients; media reports; and Kitson's autobiography.

5 Gail Dobney, interview with author, London, July 24, 2020. Dobney worked as a typesetter and designer during the 1970s and has recently retired from the position of Trades Union Congress regional secretary.

6 François Jarrige, "The Gender of the Machine, Printing Workers and Mechanical Typesetting (France, England, 1840–1880)," *Revue d'histoire moderne et contemporaine* 54–1, no. 1 (2007): 193–221, https://doi.org/10.3917 /rhmc.541.0193.

7 William E. Fredeman, "Emily Faithfull and the Victoria Press: An Experiment in Sociological Bibliography," *The Library*, 5th ser., v. 29, no. 2 (1974): 139–64.

8 Mary Davis, "Women at Work," *Britain at Work 1945–1995* (London: Metropolitan University, 2012), http://www.unionhistory .info/britainatwork/narrativedisplay.php?type =womenatwork.

9 Guerriero R. Wilson, "Women's Work in Offices and the Preservation of Men's 'Breadwinning' Jobs in Early Twentieth-Century Glasgow," *Women's History Review* 10, no. 3 (2001): 463–82, https://doi.org/10.1080/09612020100200296.

10 "Sex Discrimination Act," Jargon Buster, WorkSmart, Trades Union Congress, 2018, https://worksmart.org.uk/jargon-buster/sex -discrimination-act.

11 Kitson, *Where Sixpence Lives*.

12 Hansard, API.Parliament.UK, UK Parliament, United Kingdom, *Parliamentary Debates*, HC, January 28, 1974 (Robin Chichester-Clark), https://api.parliament.uk/historic-hansard /written-answers/1974/jan/28/average -wage#column_30w.

13 By Women for Women, "Super Services," advertisement, *Spare Rib*, October 1976, 36, https://journalarchives.jisc.ac.uk/media_open /pdf/generated/sparerib/P.523_344_Issue51 /PDF/P.523_344_Issue51_0036_98.pdf; "IBM Typesetting by Caroline MacKechnie/Shirley Divers," advertisement, *Spare Rib*, October 1976, 36, https://journalarchives.jisc.ac.uk/media _open/pdf/generated/sparerib/P.523_344 _Issue51/PDF/P.523_344_Issue51_0036_98. pdf; Judy Greenway, "Helen Lowe Obituary," *The Guardian*, August 25, 2011, https://www .theguardian.com/theguardian/2011/aug/25 /helen-lowe-obituary; Cartmail, interview.

14 Cartmail, interview.

15 Denis Herbstein, "Norma Kitson," *The Guardian*, July 12, 2002, https://www .theguardian.com/news/2002/jul/12 /guardianobituaries.

16 Kitson, *Where Sixpence Lives*, 220.

17 Kitson, *Where Sixpence Lives*, 234.

18 Cartmail, interview.

19 Gail Cartmail, email message to author, July 23, 2020.

20 Cartmail, interview.

21 Radical & Community Printshops Wiki, "Red Lion Setters."

22 Gavin Brown, "Viva Carol, Our Convenor. No One Tougher, No One Meaner," Non Stop Against Apartheid, October 19, 2019, https://nonstopagainstapartheid.wordpress.com/2019/10/19/viva-carol-our-convenor-no-one-tougher-no-one-meaner/; FRFI, "A Revolutionary Life: Carol Brickley, 26 October 1947–16 September 2019," Fight Racism, Britain, Revolutionary Communist Group, September 30, 2019, https://www.revolutionarycommunist.org/britain/fight-racism/5685-a-revolutionary-life-carol-brickley-26-october-1947-16-september-2019.

23 Helen Yaffe, email message to author, September 29, 2020.

24 Back issues of *Fight Racism! Fight Imperialism!* are available at https://www.revolutionarycommunist.org/our-paper.

25 Gavin Brown, email message to author, September 29, 2020.

26 "David Kitson Released," South African History Online, May 11, 1984, https://www.sahistory.org.za/dated-event/david-kitson-released; FRFI, "Smash Apartheid Now! The Free Steve Kitson Campaign," South Africa, Africa, Revolutionary Communist Group, February 7, 2019, https://www.revolutionarycommunist.org/africa/south-africa/5500-saa-070319.

27 FRFI, "Smash Apartheid Now!"

28 Brown, "Viva Carol."

29 Brown, email.

30 Mary Kelly, "On the Passage of a Few People through a Rather Brief Period of Time" (conversation at Tate Modern, London, March 26, 2015), https://www.tate.org.uk/search?q=mary+kelly, 11.

31 "About *m/f* a Feminist Journal," *m/f: a feminist journal*, https://www.mffeministjournal.co.uk/about-mf-a-feminist-journal; Elizabeth Cowie, email message to author, October, 18, 2020.

32 Cowie, email.

33 Kitson, *Where Sixpence Lives*, 320.

34 "Norma Kitson," *The Times*, June 17, 2002; Herbstein, "Norma Kitson."

Quick and Correct Compositors at the Case

1 Mary Beth Ferrante, "The Pressure Is Real for Working Mothers," *Forbes*, August 27, 2018, https://www.forbes.com/sites/marybethferrante/2018/08/27/the-pressure-is-real-for-working-mothers; Hana Schank and Elizabeth Wallace, "When Women Choose Children over a Career," *The Atlantic*, December 19 2016, https://www.theatlantic.com/business/archive/2016/12/opting-out/500018/; Brandie Kendrick, "2020 Will Be the Death of the Working Mother," Scary Mommy, July 23, 2020, https://www.scarymommy.com/2020-will-be-the-death-of-the-working-mother/.

2 Elizabeth Williams Anthony Dexter, *Colonial Women of Affairs: Women in Business and the Professions in America before 1776* (1924; repr., New York: A. M. Kelley, 1972).

3 Dexter, *Colonial Women of Affairs*, 33.

4 Richard Demeter, *Primer, Presses, and Composing Sticks: Women Printers of the Colonial Period* (Hicksville, NY: Exposition Press, 1979).

5 Joseph Blumenthal, *The Printed Book in America* (Hanover, NH: Published for Dartmouth College by University Press of New England, 1989), 13.

6 Lawrence C. Wroth, *The Colonial Printer* (New York: Dover, 1995), 16.

7 Blumenthal, *Printed Book in America*, 13.

8 Corydon Ireland, "Harvard's First Impressions," *Harvard Gazette*, March 8, 2015, https://news.harvard.edu/gazette/story/2012/03/harvards-first-impressions.

9 Demeter, *Primer, Presses, and Composing Sticks*, 8.

10 Demeter, *Primer, Presses, and Composing Sticks*, 13.

11 Demeter, *Primer, Presses, and Composing Sticks*, 68.

12 Demeter, *Primer, Presses, and Composing Sticks*, 32.

13 "Mary Katherine Goddard (1738–1816)," Archives of Maryland (Biographical Series), last updated July 26, 2012, http://msa.maryland.gov/megafile/msa/speccol/sc3500/sc3520/002800/002809/html/2809bio.html.

Dora Pritchett, Dora Laing, Patricia Saunders…: The Invisible Women of Monotype's Type Drawing Office

1 Alice Savoie, "The Women behind Times New Roman: The Contribution of Type Drawing Offices to Twentieth Century Type-Making," *Journal of Design History* 33, no. 3 (September 2020): 212, https://academic.oup.com/jdh/article/33/3/209/5867210.

2 British grammar schools are state secondary schools that select students through an examination, with a particular focus on academic subjects. It was and (in some quarters) still is assumed that British grammar schools provide a higher level of education for pupils than secondary schools.

3 Savoie, " Women behind Times," 212–15. Records indicate that Dora Pritchett joined the company in 1908 and that she was still working for Monotype in 1937. Laing worked for Monotype for forty-four years, from 1922 until her retirement in 1966.

4 The hot-metal Monotype system required that all letters share one of eighteen given widths, so that all letters could be neatly arranged into a matrix-case.

5 C. Poore to J. Goulding, October 5, 1950, Monotype archives. These archives, formerly located in Salfords, Surrey, UK, have been placed in storage indefinitely, as of this writing.

6 Monotype Corporation, "Monotype Matrices in the Making," *Monotype Recorder* 40, no. 3 (1956), 3–4.

7 Patricia Saunders, interview by the authors, July 28, 2018.

8 David Saunders, "Two Decades of Change: 1965–1986," *Monotype Recorder, One Hundred Years of Type Making 1897–1997*, New Series, no. 10 (1997), 29.

9 Saunders, interview.

10 Monotype Typography Ltd., Columbus type specimen (1992), 1.

11 Martha Scotford, "Messy History vs. Neat History: Toward an Expanded View of Women in Graphic Design," *Visible Language* 28, no. 4 (Autumn 1994): 367.

Press On!—Feminist Historiography of Print Culture and Collective Organizing

1 Distaff Side, "Introduction," in *Bookmaking on the Distaff Side* (San Francisco: Distaff Side, 1937), n.p.

2 Kathleen Walkup, "The Book as a Pot-Luck Offering: Edna Beilenson, Jane Grabhorn & the Books of the Distaff Side," in *Natural Enemies of Books—A Messy History of Women in Printing and Typography*, ed. MMS (London: Occasional Papers, 2020), 25–50.

3 Jane Grabhorn, "A Typographic Discourse for the Distaff Side of Printing, a Book by Ladies," in *Bookmaking on the Distaff Side* (San Francisco: Distaff Side, 1937), n.p.

4 Martha Scotford, "Messy History vs. Neat History: Toward an Expanded View of Women in Graphic Design," *Visible Language* 28, no. 4 (1994): 368–88.

5 Ulla Wikander, "The Battle between Men and Women in the Typography Trade," in *Natural Enemies of Books—A Messy History of Women in Printing and Typography*, ed. MMS (London: Occasional Papers, 2020), 107.

6 Wikander, "Battle between Men and Women," 107.

7 In 1846, the Stockholm Society for Typographers (Stockholms typografiska förening) was established, which transformed into the Swedish Association for Typographers (Svenska typografförbundet) in 1886.

8 Nils Wessel, *Typografiska Föreningen i Stockholm 1846–1926: Minnesskrift med anledning av åttioårsjubileet* (Stockholm: Typografiska föreningen, 1926), 412. All translations from Swedish to English are done by the authors.

9 Elin Johansson, *Typografiska Kvinnoklubben 1904–1939* (Stockholm: Typografiska föreningen, 1939), 93–115.

10 Hugo Lagerström, "Suffragetterna ha ej vunnit regeringen. Kvinnor dåliga som typografer. Kroppslig egenart nödvändiggör skydd," *Dagens Nyheter*, February 16, 1931.

11 Johansson, *Typografiska Kvinnoklubben*, 64.

12 See Inger Humlesjö, "Manlighetskonstruktion i arbetarhistoria och fackföreningar," *Häften För Kritiska Studier* 31, no. 3 (1998): 3–13 and Wikander, "Battle between Men and Women," 114.

13 Wikander, "Battle between Men and Women," 114.

14 MMS, "Excerpt from a Conversation with Megan Dobney," in *Natural Enemies of Books—A Messy History of Women in Printing and Typography*, ed. MMS (London: Occasional Papers, 2020), 157.

15 Jess Baines, "A Darn Good Idea: Feminist Printers and the Women's Liberation Movement in Britain," in *Natural Enemies of Books—A Messy History of Women in Printing and Typography*, ed. MMS (London: Occasional Papers, 2020), 81.

16 For an example from the private press movement, see Ida Börjel, "The Vampire and the Darling Priest of Modernism," in *Natural Enemies of Books—A Messy History of Women in Printing and Typography*, ed. MMS (London: Occasional Papers, 2020), 61–74.

17 Angela McRobbie, *Be Creative: Making a Living in the New Culture Industries* (Cambridge, UK: Polity Press, 2016).

18 Kleines Postfordistisches Drama, "A Comment by Kleines Postfordistisches Drama," in *Casco Issues XII: Generous Structures*, ed. Binna Choi and Axel Wieder (Utrecht and New York/Berlin: Casco and Sternberg Press, 2011), 49–55.

▬

Celebrating Söre Popitz, the Bauhaus's Only Known Woman Advertising Designer

1 For an account of weaving activities at the Bauhaus, see T'ai Smith, *Bauhaus Weaving Theory: From Feminine Craft to Mode of Design* (Minneapolis: University of Minnesota Press, 2014).

2 Söre Popitz diary, Irmgard Sörensen-Popitz Estate, Stiftung Bauhaus Dessau, Dessau, Germany. Thank you to Steffen Schröter for helping me to access these materials.

3 Steffen Schröter, interview by author, December 2018. See also Steffen Schröter, "Die Künstlerin und Werbegrafikerin Irmgard Sörensen-Popitz. Entwicklung eines Ausstellungskonzeptes auf der Grundlage ihres Nachlasses in der Stiftung Bauhaus Dessau" (bachelor's thesis, Leipzig, 2014).

4 Patrick Rössler, "Eine vergessene Pionierin— Irmgard Sörensen-Popitz, Art Direktorin im Beyer-Verlag," in *Women in Graphic Design* 1890–2012, ed. Gerda Breuer and Julia Meer (Berlin: Jovis, 2012), 123.

5 Söre Popitz diary.

6 László Moholy-Nagy, *Von Material zu Architektur* (Munich: Langen, 1929), 153.

7 Söre Popitz diary.

8 Söre Popitz diary.

9 On this topic, see Anja Baumhoff, *The Gendered World of the Bauhaus: The Politics of Power at the Weimar Republic's Premier Art Institute, 1919–1932* (Frankfurt am Main: Peter Lang, 2001).

10 Söre Popitz diary.

11 For more on the magazine, see Patrick Rössler,

Die neue Linie 1929–1943: das Bauhaus am Kiosk (Bielefeld: Kerber, 2007).

12 Rössler, "Eine vergessene Pionierin," 126.

13 Steffen Schröter, interview by author.

▬

Clearing the Fog: Marget Larsen, San Francisco Designer

1 Roger Black, email message to author, October 7, 2020.

2 The bio for an exhibition of De Patta's work that took place at the Museum of Art and Design in 2012 noted that, along with her industrial designer husband, she sought to promote the Bauhaus design philosophy and its democratic social agenda in the Bay Area through a host of creative endeavors, including a production line of affordable modernist jewelry and several educational ventures.

3 Cyril Magnin and Cynthia Robins, *Call Me Cyril* (New York: McGraw-Hill, 1981), 118.

4 Patrick Coyne, email message to author, October 7, 2020.

5 Steven Heller, "Born Modern," *Eye*, Autumn 1993, http://www.eyemagazine.com/feature /article/born-modern.

6 Bob Skillicorn, "Redesigning the Newspaper for the Needs of the Readers," *Press Democrat* (Santa Rosa, California), September 12, 1977.

7 Joan Didion, *Slouching Towards Bethlehem* (New York: Farrar, Straus and Giroux, 1968), 5.

8 Alison Isenberg, *Designing San Francisco: Art, Land, and Urban Renewal in the City by the Bay* (Princeton, NJ: Princeton University Press, 2017), 55.

9 Grey Advertising, advertisement for Canada Dry, 1968; possibly Leo Burnett Co., advertisement for Dash Detergent, Procter & Gamble, 1967.

10 "Super SuperGraphics," *San Francisco Examiner*, June 27, 1971.

▬

Betti Broadwater Haft: "Letterforms Are Sacred to Me"

1 All quotations in this text are taken from interviews between Betti Haft and the author between July 3, 2018, and August 26, 2020.

Contributors

Sean Adams is the chair of the undergraduate and graduate Graphic Design programs at ArtCenter College of Design. He is the author of multiple books and an on-screen author for LinkedIn Learning. He is the only two-term AIGA national president in AIGA's hundred-year history. In 2014, Adams was awarded the AIGA Medal, the highest honor in the profession. He writes for Design Observer and is on its editorial board. Adams is an AIGA and Aspen Institute fellow. He has been widely recognized by major competitions and publications and has had a solo exhibition at the San Francisco Museum of Modern Art. Adams was a founding partner at AdamsMorioka.

Tasheka Arceneaux-Sutton is an associate professor of graphic design at Southeastern Louisiana University and faculty at Vermont College of Fine Art; she also taught typography at Loyola Marymount University. She is the principal of BlacVoice Graphic Design Studio, which specializes in branding, electronic media, identity, illustration, print, and publication design, providing design services for educational institutions, nonprofit organizations, and small businesses. She earned an MFA in graphic design from California Institute of the Arts and a BA from Loyola University New Orleans. Her research involves discovering Black people who have made significant contributions to the design profession but have been excluded from graphic design history.

Tereza Bettinardi is a graphic designer based in São Paulo. She studied journalism and graduated in graphic design from Universidade Federal de Santa Maria. Since 2014, she has run her own studio, working on projects from editorial design to visual identity. She had taught at a few of the major design schools in São Paulo. In 2014, she cofounded A Escola Livre (the Free School, 2014–18), an independent educational project in design education involved in the coordination and conception of various activities, including workshops, book publishing, and open interviews with design professionals.

Anne Galperin is an associate professor of graphic design at the State University of New York at New Paltz, where she teaches courses on design history and design research methods. Galperin earned her MFA in 2D design from Cranbrook Academy of Art and her BSc in human development and social policy from Northwestern University. Her presentations include FORMA (Cuba), SHOT (Society for the History of Technology), the AIGA Design Educators Conferences, and the Design History Society, among others. Galperin is currently researching and writing a book about functional wearables.

175

Meredith James is an associate professor in the graphic design program at Portland State University. Her research is focused on design theory and how to develop a culture of design that is more reflective, equitable, humanist, and self-aware. James has presented her work across the United States and Europe, speaking in cities such as New York, Los Angeles, Brighton, and Paris. Her writing was recently published in *Ethics in Design* and *Communication: Critical Perspectives*. James received her MFA from Cranbrook Academy of Art.

Katie Krcmarik has worked as both a graphic designer and educator for two decades. She has worked in a variety of design positions including in a studio, in house for a variety of companies, and as a freelance graphic designer. Krcmarik currently teaches and coordinates the visual communications foundational courses for the College of Journalism and Mass Communications at the University of Nebraska–Lincoln. She previously taught graphic design at Mott Community College for eleven years as an adjunct faculty member in the Fine Arts and Social Sciences departments.

Briar Levit is an associate professor of graphic design at Portland State University. She earned her undergraduate degree from San Francisco State University and her master's degree from Central Saint Martins College of Art & Design. Since directing and producing *Graphic Means: A History of Graphic Design Production* (2017), she has become very focused on helping to expand the graphic design history dialogue and canon. Currently, she is working with Louise Sandhaus (California Institute of the Arts) on The People's Graphic Design Archive, a crowdsourced, online graphic design archive that helps preserve design while expanding notions of who has made good and important work.

Ian Lynam works at the intersection of graphic design, design education, and design theory. He is faculty at Temple University Japan, Vermont College of Fine Arts, and Meme Design School and is a visiting critic at California Institute of the Arts. He writes regularly for *IDEA* (Japan), *Slanted* (Denmark), and *Modes of Criticism* (Portugal), exploring critical feminist/internationalist perspectives on design and culture. He operates the Tokyo-based publishing imprint and type foundry Wordshape as well as a design studio.

Sarah McCoy is a full-time associate professor of graphic design at Drake University. She also owns the Permanent Collection Letterpress + Design Studio, located in downtown Des Moines, Iowa. She designs and prints all of her products, working for varied clients such as Madsen Cycles, Paper Source, and the University of Southern California. McCoy received an MFA in graphic design in 2005 from the University of Iowa. In 2006, she received a graduate certificate from the UI Center for the Book. McCoy has been actively printing since 2002, exhibiting work, and leading letterpress workshops both nationally and internationally—most recently with ATypI in Antwerp, Belgium. Her design and letterpress work has been featured in numerous publications. Her artist books are included in many university special collections, including those of Yale, Wellesley, and Stanford.

MMS is graphic designers Maryam Fanni, Matilda Flodmark, and Sara Kaaman, who have collaborated since 2012 on investigations and writings on visual culture with a focus on feminism and workers' history. In 2020, they published the book *Natural Enemies of Books: A Messy History of Women in Printing and Typography* (Occasional Papers). The book is a response to the groundbreaking 1937 publication *Bookmaking on the Distaff Side*, which brought together contributions by women printers, illustrators, authors, typographers, and typesetters. It highlights the print industry's inequalities and proposes a takeover of the history of the book.

Madeleine Morley is a design and art writer from London based in Berlin. Her writing has appeared in *Dazed and Confused* magazine, *The Observer*, *AnOther* magazine, *032c*, *Elephant*, *Eye* magazine, *Creative Review*, and many other publications. She was previously editor of *magCulture* journal and is currently an editor at *AIGA Eye on Design* magazine. She lectures regularly on design and media.

Fiona Ross specializes in type design and typography, primarily for Arabic, South Asian, and Thai scripts. Ross has a background in languages and a PhD in Indian paleography from SOAS. She is a part-time professor in type design at the Department of Typography and Graphic Communication at the University of Reading, UK, and a typographic consultant, type designer, and author. Her most recent design work has been in collaboration with John Hudson and Neelakash Kshetrimayum for clients Harvard University Press and *Anandabazar Patrika*. For her work in type design and education, Ross received the SoTA Typography Award (2014) and the Type Directors Club Medal (2018).

Louise Sandhaus is a graphic designer and faculty in the Graphic Design Program at California Institute of the Arts (CalArts). She is the author/designer of *Earthquakes, Mudslides, Fires and Riots: California and Graphic Design 1936–1986* (2014) and co-author/co-designer of *A Colorful Life: Gere Kavanaugh, Designer* (2018). Sandhaus is founder and codirector of the People's Graphic Design Archive, a crowdsourced virtual archive representing an expansive graphic design history. Her work is in the permanent collection of the San Francisco Museum of Modern Art and the Bibliothèque nationale de France, Paris.

Alice Savoie is an independent type designer and researcher based in Lyon, France. She holds an MA and a PhD from the University of Reading. As a practicing type designer, she has collaborated with international foundries and design studios. Her recent type design work includes Faune, an award-winning typeface family for the French Centre national des arts plastiques. She is currently a postdoctoral researcher on the Leverhulme-funded Women in Type research project at the University of Reading. She teaches type design at ANRT Nancy (France) and ÉCAL (Switzerland).

Martha Scotford is professor emerita of graphic design at the College of Design at North Carolina State University and the author of *Cipe Pineles: a Life of Design*.

Ruth Sykes is a graphic designer, lecturer, and design historian based in London. She has written about the history of women in graphic design for publications including the London Transport Museum's book *Poster Girls*, the *AIGA Eye on Design*, and *TypoGraphic*, the journal of the International Society of Typographic Designers. Sykes curated and organized two exhibitions of work by female graphic designers, held at Central Saint Martins, in collaboration with the Central Saint Martins Museum & Study Collection. Her teaching frames graphic design as both socially engaged practice and research method, and she currently teaches final-year undergraduate graphic design students at Central

Saint Martins. Her design practice is socially located, collaborating with clients from charity, education, and arts sectors, designing publications and visual identities. Sykes gained undergraduate degrees in history (Sussex) and graphic design (Central Saint Martins) and a master's degree in the history of design (Royal College of Art). She is a fellow of the Higher Education Academy.

Aggie Toppins is an associate professor and chair of design at the Sam Fox School of Design and Visual Arts at Washington University in St. Louis. Previously, she taught at the University of Tennessee at Chattanooga, where she served as the first female department head in art. Toppins is interested in the roles of critical theory, history, and social justice in studio-based making. She holds a BS in graphic design from the University of Cincinnati College of Design, Architecture, Art, and Planning and an MFA from the Maryland Institute College of Art.

Linda M. Waggoner is an independent scholar and former faculty member of American multicultural studies at Sonoma State University, California. She specializes in Great Lakes Métis and Ho-Chunk history and is a consultant in Native American genealogy. Her publications include *Fire Light: The Life of Angel De Cora, Winnebago Artist* (University of Oklahoma Press, 2008) and *Starring Red Wing: The Incredible Career of Lilian M. St. Cyr, the First Native American Film Star* (University of Nebraska Press, 2019).

Credits

*Photographers are unknown
unless otherwise noted.*

Cover
Bottom left: Art and design
created by Louise E. Jefferson,
permission granted by Friendship
Press, Inc., on behalf of the
National Council of Churches in
the USA; center right: Copyright
Stiftung Bauhaus Dessau; bottom
right: Reprinted by permission
from House Industries

2: Monotype archives

Introduction
9: Library of Congress;
10: Copyright Stiftung Bauhaus
Dessau; 11: Bea Feitler Papers,
the New School Archives and
Special Collection, the New
School, New York, NY

**"Her Greatest Work Lay in
Decorative Design"**
12–21: Author's collection

A Black Renaissance Woman
22–27: Art and design created
by Louise E. Jefferson, permission
granted by Friendship Press, Inc.,
on behalf of the National Council
of Churches in the USA; 28:
Copyright of the National Urban
League. All Rights Reserved.
Reproduced with the permission
of the National Urban League

**Women of the Federal Art
Project Poster Division**
32–41: Library of Congress

One for the Books
42–51: Courtesy of Ellen Raskin
Estate; 47–49: Ellen Raskin
Papers, Children's Literature
Research Collections, University
of Minnesota Libraries

Bea Feitler
52, 60–61: Kellan Design Archive,
the New School Archives and
Special Collection, the New
School, New York, NY; 54–56:
Bea Feitler Papers, the New
School Archives and Special
Collection, the New School, New
York, NY

By Women, for Women
62: Courtesy of Palczewski
Suffrage Postcard Archive;
64–65: Schlesinger Library,
Radcliffe Institute, Harvard
University; 67: Emory Center
for Digital Scholarship, Emory
University; 69: Suffrage
Collection, Sophia Smith
Collection, Smith College;
70: Social Welfare History
Project, James Branch Cabell
Library, Virginia Commonwealth
University Libraries

**Collective Authorship and
Shared Process**
84–91: Courtesy of Mary Patten

Typist to Typesetter
94: Revolutionary Communist
Group "Our Paper" online collection; 96: City of London Anti-
Apartheid Group Archive (CAAG)
Bishopsgate Institute Archives;
101: *m/f: a feminist journal* online
collection

**Quick and Correct Compositors
at the Case**
102: Library of Congress;
103: Photograph by Sarah McCoy,
International Printing Museum,
Carson, California; 104: © The
Metropolitan Museum of Art,
New York, NY, Rogers Fund,
1926. Source: Art Resource,
New York, NY

**Dora Pritchett, Dora Laing,
Patricia Saunders…**
110: The Monotype Recorder
40, no. 3: 4; 113: Richard Cooper
personal archives; 112, 115–17:
Monotype archives

Press On!
120–22: Courtesy Arbark—
Arbetarrörelsens arkiv och
bibliotek (Swedish Labor
Movement's Archives and
Library), Stockholm, Sweden

Celebrating Söre Popitz
128–36: Copyright Stiftung
Bauhaus Dessau

Clearing the Fog
137: Courtesy Ellen Magnin
Newman, photograph by
Benjamin Blackwell; 140–47:
Courtesy of *Communication Arts*
magazine

Betti Broadwater Haft
150: Courtesy of College of
Staten Island: 155: Will Burtin
Papers, RIT Cary Graphic Design
Archives; 156: Reprinted by per-
mission from House Industries;
159: Photograph by Anne
Galperin, courtesy of Betti Haft

160: Courtesy of Ellen Raskin
Estate; 181: Art and design
created by Louise E. Jefferson,
permission granted by Friendship
Press, Inc., on behalf of the
National Council of Churches in
the USA; 184: Courtesy of Mary
Patten; 189: Library of Congress

Index

Louise E. Jefferson, illustration for *We Sing America*, 1936.

WE SING
AMERICA

BY MARION CUTHBERT

ILLUSTRATIONS BY LOUISE E. JEFFERSON

FRIENDSHIP PRESS
NEW YORK

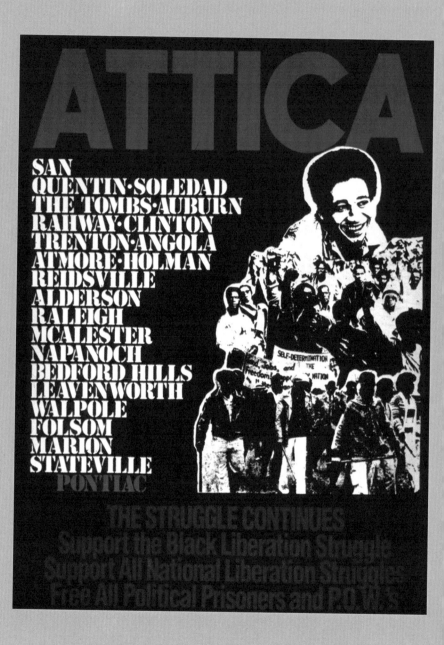

ATTICA

SAN
QUENTIN·SOLEDAD
THE TOMBS·AUBURN
RAHWAY·CLINTON
TRENTON·ANGOLA
ATMORE·HOLMAN
REIDSVILLE
ALDERSON
RALEIGH
MCALESTER
NAPANOCH
BEDFORD HILLS
LEAVENWORTH
WALPOLE
FOLSOM
MARION
STATEVILLE
PONTIAC

THE STRUGGLE CONTINUES
Support the Black Liberation Struggle
Support All National Liberation Struggles
Free All Political Prisoners and P.O.W.'s

Madame Binh Graphics Collective, *Attica: The Struggle Continues***, 1978, poster.**

The Unanimous Declaration of the Thirteen United States of America, printed by Mary Katharine Goddard, 1777.

In CONGRESS, July 4, 1776.

THE UNANIMOUS

DECLARATION

OF THE

Thirteen United States of America.

WHEN, in the Course of human Events, it becomes necessary for one People to dissolve the Political Bands which have connected them with another, and to assume, among the Powers of the Earth, the separate and equal Station to which the Laws of Nature and of Nature's GOD entitle them, a decent Respect to the Opinions of Mankind requires that they should declare the Causes which impel them to the Separation.

We hold these Truths to be self-evident, that all Men are created equal, that they are endowed, by their CREATOR, with certain unalienable Rights, that among these are Life, Liberty, and the Pursuit of Happiness.—That to secure these Rights, Governments are instituted among Men, deriving their just Powers from the Consent of the Governed, that whenever any Form of Government becomes destructive of these Ends, it is the Right of the People to alter or to abolish it, and to institute new Government, laying its Foundation on such Principles, and organizing its Powers in such Form, as to them shall seem most likely to effect their Safety and Happiness. Prudence, indeed, will dictate, that Governments long established, should not be changed for light and transient Causes; and accordingly all Experience hath shewn, that Mankind are more disposed to suffer, while Evils are sufferable, than to right themselves by abolishing the Forms to which they are accustomed. But when a long Train of Abuses and Usurpations, pursuing invariably the same Object, evinces a Design to reduce them under absolute Despotism, it is their Right, it is their Duty, to throw off such Government, and to provide new Guards for their future Security. Such has been the patient Sufferance of these Colonies; and such is now the Necessity which constrains them to alter their former Systems of Government. The History of the present King of Great-Britain is a History of repeated Injuries and Usurpations, all having in direct Object the Establishment of an absolute Tyranny over these States. To prove this, let Facts be submitted to a candid World.

He has refused his Assent to Laws, the most wholesome and necessary for the public Good.

He has forbidden his Governors to pass Laws of immediate and pressing Importance, unless suspended in their Operation till his Assent should be obtained; and when so suspended, he has utterly neglected to attend to them.

He has refused to pass other Laws for the Accommodation of large Districts of People, unless those People would relinquish the Right of Representation in the Legislature, a Right inestimable to them, and formidable to Tyrants only.

He has called together Legislative Bodies at Places unusual, uncomfortable, and distant from the Depository of their public Records, for the sole Purpose of fatiguing them into Compliance with his Measures.

He has dissolved Representative Houses repeatedly, for opposing with manly Firmness his Invasions on the Rights of the People.

He has refused for a long Time, after such Dissolutions, to cause others to be elected; whereby the Legislative Powers, incapable of Annihilation, have returned to the People at large for their exercise; the State remaining, in the mean Time, exposed to all the Dangers of Invasion from without, and Convulsions within.

He has endeavoured to prevent the Population of these States; for that Purpose obstructing the Laws for Naturalization of Foreigners; refusing to pass others to encourage their Migrations hither, and raising the Conditions of new Appropriations of Lands.

He has obstructed the Administration of Justice, by refusing his Assent to Laws for establishing Judiciary Powers.

He has made Judges dependent on his Will alone, for the Tenure of their Offices, and the Amount and Payment of their Salaries.

He has erected a Multitude of new Offices, and sent hither Swarms of Officers to harrass our People, and eat out their Substance.

He has kept among us, in Times of Peace, Standing Armies, without the Consent of our Legislatures.

He has affected to render the Military independent of and superior to the Civil Power.

He has combined with others to subject us to a Jurisdiction foreign to our Constitution, and unacknowledged by our Laws; giving his Assent to their Acts of pretended Legislation:

For quartering large Bodies of Armed Troops among us:

For protecting them, by a mock Trial, from Punishment for any Murders which they should commit on the Inhabitants of these States:

For cutting off our Trade with all Parts of the World:

For imposing Taxes on us without our Consent:

For depriving us, in many Cases, of the Benefits of Trial by Jury:

For transporting us beyond Seas to be tried for pretended Offences:

For abolishing the free System of English Laws in a neighbouring Province, establishing therein an arbitrary Government, and enlarging its Boundaries, so as to render it at once an Example and fit Instrument for introducing the same absolute Rule into these Colonies:

For taking away our Charters, abolishing our most valuable Laws, and altering fundamentally the Forms of our Governments:

For suspending our own Legislatures, and declaring themselves invested with Power to legislate for us in all Cases whatsoever.

He has abdicated Government here, by declaring us out of his Protection and waging War against us.

He has plundered our Seas, ravaged our Coasts, burnt our Towns, and destroyed the Lives of our People.

He is, at this Time, transporting large Armies of foreign Mercenaries to complete the Works of Death, Desolation, and Tyranny, already begun with Circumstances of Cruelty and Perfidy, scarcely paralleled in the most barbarous Ages, and totally unworthy the Head of a civilized Nation.

He has constrained our Fellow-Citizens, taken Captive on the high Seas, to bear Arms against their Country, to become the Executioners of their Friends and Brethren, or to fall themselves by their Hands.

He has excited domestic Insurrections amongst us, and has endeavoured to bring on the Inhabitants of our Frontiers, the merciless Indian Savages, whose known Rule of Warfare, is an undistinguished Destruction, of all Ages, Sexes, and Conditions.

In every Stage of these Oppressions we have Petitioned for Redress in the most humble Terms: Our repeated Petitions have been answered only by repeated Injury. A Prince, whose Character is thus marked by every Act which may define a Tyrant, is unfit to be the Ruler of a free People.

Nor have we been wanting in Attentions to our British Brethren. We have warned them, from Time to Time, of Attempts by their Legislature to extend an unwarrantable Jurisdiction over us. We have reminded them of the Circumstances of our Emigration and Settlement here. We have appealed to their native Justice and Magnanimity, and we have conjured them by the Ties of our common Kindred to disavow these Usurpations, which would inevitably interrupt our Connections and Correspondence. They too have been deaf to the Voice of Justice and of Consanguinity. We must, therefore, acquiesce in the Necessity, which denounces our Separation, and hold them, as we hold the Rest of Mankind, Enemies in War, in Peace Friends.

We, therefore, the Representatives of the UNITED STATES OF AMERICA, in GENERAL CONGRESS Assembled, appealing to the Supreme Judge of the World for the Rectitude of our Intentions, do, in the Name, and by Authority of the good People of these Colonies, solemnly Publish and Declare, That these United Colonies are, and of Right ought to be, FREE AND INDEPENDENT STATES; that they are absolved from all Allegiance to the British Crown, and that all political Connection between them and the State of Great-Britain, is, and ought to be, totally dissolved; and that as FREE AND INDEPENDENT STATES, they have full Power to levy War, conclude Peace, contract Alliances, establish Commerce, and to do all other Acts and Things which INDEPENDENT STATES may of Right do. And for the Support of this Declaration, with a firm Reliance on the Protection of DIVINE PROVIDENCE, we mutually pledge to each other our Lives, our Fortunes, and our sacred Honour.

John Hancock.

GEORGIA	Button Gwinnett, Lyman Hall, Geo. Walton.		
NORTH-CAROLINA	Wm. Hooper, Joseph Hewes, John Penn.		
SOUTH-CAROLINA	Edward Rutledge, Thos. Heyward, junr. Thomas Lynch, junr. Arthur Middleton.		
MARYLAND	Samuel Chase, Wm. Paca, Thos. Stone, Charles Carroll, of Carrollton.		
VIRGINIA	George Wythe, Richard Henry Lee, Tho. Jefferson, Benja. Harrison, Thos. Nelson, jr. Francis Lightfoot Lee, Carter Braxton.		
PENNSYLVANIA	Robt. Morris, Benjamin Rush, Benja. Franklin, John Morton, Geo. Clymer, Jas. Smith, Geo. Taylor, James Wilson, Geo. Ross.		
DELAWARE	Cæsar Rodney, Geo. Read.		
NEW-YORK	Wm. Floyd, Phil. Livingston, Frans. Lewis, Lewis Morris.		
NEW-JERSEY	Richd. Stockton, Jno. Witherspoon, Frans. Hopkinson, John Hart, Abra. Clark.		
NEW-HAMPSHIRE	Josiah Bartlett, Wm. Whipple, Matthew Thornton.		
MASSACHUSETTS-BAY	Saml. Adams, John Adams, Robt. Treat Paine, Elbridge Gerry.		
RHODE-ISLAND AND PROVIDENCE, &c.	Step. Hopkins, William Ellery.		
CONNECTICUT	Roger Sherman, Saml. Huntington, Wm. Williams, Oliver Wolcott.		

In CONGRESS, January 18, 1777.

ORDERED,

THAT an authenticated Copy of the DECLARATION of INDEPENDENCY, with the Names of the MEMBERS of CONGRESS, subscribing the same, be sent to each of the UNITED STATES, and that they be desired to have the same put on RECORD.

By Order of CONGRESS,

JOHN HANCOCK, President.

Attest. Chas. Thomson, Secy.   A True Copy,
John Hancock, Presid.

BALTIMORE, in MARYLAND: Printed by MARY KATHARINE GODDARD.

Study the Old,
but Create the New

—Varvara Stepanova